J.D. GREEAR
WITH CURRICULUM BY
SPENCE SHELTON

THE GOSPEL ACCORDING TO JONAH
A NEW KIND OF OBEDIENCE

LifeWay Press®
Nashville, Tennessee

PRODUCTION TEAM

WRITER:

Spence Shelton

EDITORIAL PROJECT LEADER:

Brian Daniel

ART DIRECTOR & DESIGNER:

Jon Rodda

CONTENT EDITOR:

Brian Gass

PRODUCTION EDITOR:

Juliana Duncan

VIDEO PRODUCER & EDITOR:

Hal Sandifer

VIDEO DIRECTOR:

Lisa Turner

DIRECTOR, ADULT MINISTRY:

Faith Whatley

DIRECTOR, ADULT
MINISTRY PUBLISHING:

Philip Nation

Published by LifeWay Press® • ©2013 J.D. Greear

ISBN: 9781415877807
Item: 005558799
Dewey Decimal Classification: 224.92
Subject Headings: BIBLE. O.T. JONAH \ CHRISTIAN LIFE \ EVANGELISTIC WORK

Unless otherwise noted, all Scripture quotations are taken from the Holman Christian Standard Bible®, Copyright 1999, 2000, 2002, 2003 by Holman Bible Publishers. Used by permission. Scripture quotations marked ESV are from The Holy Bible, English Standard Version copyright © 2001 by Crossway, a publishing ministry of Good News Publishers. Used by permission. All rights reserved. Scripture quotations marked MSG are from The Message, copyright © 1993, 1994, 1995, 1996, 2001, 2002 by Eugene Peterson. Published by NavPress. Used by permission. Scripture quotations marked NLT are taken from the Holy Bible, New Living Translation, copyright © 1996. Used by permission of Tyndale House Publishers, Inc., Wheaton, IL 60189 USA. All rights reserved. Scripture quotations marked NASB are taken from the New American Standard Bible®, Copyright © 1960, 1962, 1963, 1968, 1971, 1972, 1973, 1975, 1977, 1995 by The Lockman Foundation. Used by permission (www.lockman.org).

To order additional copies of this resource, order online at www.lifeway.com; write LifeWay Small Groups: One LifeWay Plaza, Nashville, TN 37234-0152; fax order to (615) 251-5933; or call toll-free (800) 458-2772.

Printed in the United States of America

Adult Ministry Publishing
LifeWay Church Resources
One LifeWay Plaza
Nashville, TN 37234-0152

CONTENTS

ABOUT THE AUTHOR

J.D. GREEAR is the lead pastor of the Summit Church, in Raleigh-Durham, NC and author of *Gospel: Recovering the Power that Made Christianity Revolutionary* (2011) and *Stop Asking Jesus into Your Heart: How to Know for Sure You Are Saved* (2013). Two main things characterize the Summit Church: its gospel focus and its sending culture. The gospel is not merely the diving board off of which we jump into the pool of Christianity, it's the pool itself. Joy, reckless generosity, and audacious faith all come by learning more about and experiencing God's extravagant love found in Christ.

God has blessed the Summit Church with tremendous growth. Under J.D.'s leadership, the Summit has grown from a plateaued church of 300 to one of more than 7,000, making it one of Outreach magazine's "top 25 fastest-growing churches in America" for several years running.

J.D. has also led the Summit to further the kingdom of God by pursuing a bold vision to plant one thousand new churches by the year 2050. In the last ten years, the church has sent out more than 300 people to serve on church planting teams, both domestically and internationally. J.D. completed his Ph.D. in Theology at Southeastern Baptist Theological Seminary where he is also a faculty member, writing on the correlations between early church presentations of the gospel and Islamic theology. Having lived serving among Muslims, he has a burden to see them, as well as every nation on earth, come to know and love the salvation of God in Christ.

He and his beautiful wife Veronica live in Raleigh, NC and are raising four ridiculously cute kids: Kharis, Alethia, Ryah, and Adon.

SPENCE SHELTON is the small groups pastor of the Summit Church. Spence found the church as a college student 10 years ago and has had the privilege to participate in the amazing movement of God taking place through the Summit in Raleigh-Durham.

Spence holds a BSBA from UNC-Chapel Hill and an M.Div in Christian Ethics from Southeastern Baptist Theological Seminary. God has given Spence a passion for leading the local church to live out its calling to be a gospel-driven, life-giving community. Spence teaches around the country on the gospel and discipleship in the local church. He's written and published several articles and small-group studies. His first book, *The People of God* co-authored with Trevor Joy, is due to be released by B&H in the spring of 2014.

Spence and his stunning wife Courtney live in Durham, NC and are the proud parents of Zeke the Wise, Ben the Brave, and Ellie the Beautiful.

WELCOME TO
THE GOSPEL ACCORDING TO JONAH

The Book of Jonah is not just about a runaway prophet and a big, magical fish. Jonah is first and foremost about a gracious God in relentless pursuit of those He loves. Yes, the Book of Jonah tells the story of a man who ran from God and was swallowed up by a fish because of that. But Jonah also puts on display the heart of a God who would pursue us even to the point of death.

You likely will see some of your own story in Jonah's. The Jewish people have a tradition on Yom Kippur—after the Book of Jonah is read the congregation stands and says in unison, "We are Jonah." This is true. But on a more profound level, we are Nineveh. We were the ones so wicked that no one could fathom why, or how, God would show us mercy. Yet God pursued us. And He cast Himself into the sea of His own wrath, entering the bowels of death for 3 days, so that we could be saved.

That is the gospel according to Jonah. Seeing that, experiencing that, produces a whole new kind of obedience in us—an obedience that comes not as a response to threats but from a heart that desires God. Gospel obedience comes not from the fear of being swallowed by fish; gospel obedience comes from seeing that God's love was so great that He would be swallowed up by death for us.

Jonah has become one of my favorite books in the Bible. Studying it brought profound changes in the church I lead and in me personally. I read it often and share it with my children. I pray it has the same effect on you. May God open your eyes to how wide, and how high, and how deep, and how long, is the love of God for you in Christ.

HOW TO USE

THE GOSPEL
ACCORDING TO
JONAH
EXPERIENCE

WELCOME to a six-week journey through the Book of Jonah that we hope will lead to a gospel-enriched experience for you personally as well as for your church. Here's how the study works:

Introduction: Each session begins with a narrative overview of the weekly topic. You will probably want to read this before your group meets so that you'll better understand the topic and the context for your time together. Summarize for those who may not have read it.

Warm-Up: Your actual group time will most likely begin here with an icebreaker that is designed to help you ease into the study and get everyone talking. Some questions for review are included to help everyone remember what was discussed in the previous session and also to allow the group to dialogue about their personal time with God the week before.

Video Setup: A brief description of J.D.'s teaching helps to set the stage for hearing from God during each 15-minute video teaching segment.

Video Guide: The video guide is an outline of the main teaching points to help you follow along with J.D. and serves as a reference point for further discussion.

Video Feedback: This part of the group experience allows everyone to make sure they got the main teaching points and gives the opportunity to process and share as a group so that you can learn from each other.

Group Discussion: These questions will help the group study passages that reinforce J.D.'s teaching in the video. Each question is designed to lead the group deeper into the gospel so that the gospel will become a part of who they are. These questions facilitate the work that the Holy Spirit is actually accomplishing in the life of the individual and the group. You may want to summarize the opening paragraph and only read key Scriptures from some of the lengthier passages.

Wrap-Up: This part of each session serves as a conclusion to the group Bible study and summarizes key points. It also offers a final challenge and a prompt to pray together. Ideas for the challenge can be found on the DVD-ROM in the Leader Kit.

Personal Study: Three devotions are included for each session. These devotions allow group members to spend more time in the Book of Jonah which will enrich the Bible study experience. QR codes can be found with several of the devotions offering further video teaching or illustration from writer and small-groups pastor Spence Shelton.

Leader Guide: The Leader Guide helps you prepare for each session and the study as a whole. The DVD-ROM includes video teaching help from Spence for each session as well as possible answers to discussion questions to help you prepare for the group discussion.

Appendix: A gospel presentation is included with the study. Group members are encouraged to make sharing the gospel a priority whether they use this appendix as a guide or another method that they are more comfortable with. Once we are saturated with the gospel, it is natural to not only live it out but to proclaim the gospel to others.

Week 1

I AM JONAH

INTRODUCTION

I love stories. I love suspending my disbelief and immersing myself in the storyline. I love trying to relate to the hero, even the tragic ones, placing myself in his shoes to ask myself what I would do in his situation. As a culture we are story-driven. If you want to communicate your message in a compelling way, get a testimony of someone whose life has been changed by your message and let them tell their story. We may or may not get your message, but we will connect with someone's story.

The Book of Jonah tells a short, fascinating story. In all of the Bible, Jonah is one character you do not want to emulate. Jonah defied God, sat in a fish belly for three days, preached to his most hated enemy, and then got into a shouting match with God. Bottom line, "WWJD" is not short for "What would Jonah do?"

Yet in Jonah we see a dangerously honest reflection of ourselves. He was a nice guy who deep down held a frustration with a God who was acting in ways Jonah couldn't believe to be fair or good. But in Jonah's story we also see a bigger story that Jonah himself missed. A story of love and grace. A story that, when understood, gives us hope that there will be more to our story than there was to Jonah's.

GROUP STUDY

Warm-Up

1. Growing up, did you have any big moments where you rebelled against your parents? What happened?

2. What forms of discipline have you seen or experienced that you are grateful for? Did you always feel that way? Explain.

Video Setup

In this session J.D. will look at Jonah's rebellion against God's command in chapter 1 of the Book of Jonah. We will hear how this depicts our own relationship with God, and how Christ meets us in our rebellion, offering us restoration instead.

Play Video 1: "Rebellion."

Video Guide

The notes below are designed to help you follow along with the video. Do not feel restricted to only these notes. We encourage you to write down other key thoughts that impact you.

Jonah had _____ _____ against Nineveh.

Rebellion is simply saying _____ to God.

If you want to _____ , there will always be a ship prepared to take you to Tarshish.

The downward progression of sin starts with _____ _____ and ends in total spiritual disaster.

Our _____ always affects others.

God sends storms into the lives of His people to wake them up from the _____ of sin.

That storm in your life is not there to _____ you back for your sin, but to _____ you back from your sin.

That storm is not designed for _____; it's designed for _____.

Video Feedback

What resonated with you from this first video session?

Looking back in your life, what has God used, like Jonah's storm, to bring you back from your sin?

 If you missed this session, you can download the video teaching from *www.lifeway.com/Jonah*

Group Discussion

DANIEL 3

Chapter 3 of the Book of Daniel recounts a well-known story which provides a helpful contrast to the opening chapter of Jonah's story. Shadrach, Meshach, and Abednego are the main characters in this story. They were all men of Jerusalem living basically as captives of Babylon. Babylon sacked Jerusalem and so they were at this point under Babylonian rule. These three guys, along with Daniel, were chosen by the king's men because they were on the Who's Who of Israel's young guys and the Hebrew Top 30 Under 30 lists. They were intelligent, handsome, and wise, and came from well-to-do backgrounds. But they got into a couple of skirmishes with the king because they refused to compromise their worship of God for favor with the king. Which brings us to chapter 3 when Shadrach, Meshach, and Abednego were given an ultimatum to either worship King Nebuchadnezzar's gods or be thrown into a fiery furnace.

Read Daniel 3:13-15

> ¹³ Then in a furious rage Nebuchadnezzar gave orders to
> bring in Shadrach, Meshach, and Abednego. So these men
> were brought before the king. ¹⁴ Nebuchadnezzar asked them,
> "Shadrach, Meshach, and Abednego, is it true that you don't
> serve my gods or worship the gold statue I have set up? ¹⁵ Now
> if you're ready, when you hear the sound of the horn, flute,
> zither, lyre, harp, drum, and every kind of music, fall down
> and worship the statue I made. But if you don't worship it, you
> will immediately be thrown into a furnace of blazing fire—
> and who is the god who can rescue you from my power?"

1. While on the surface these two stories couldn't be more different, how are the circumstances facing Shadrach, Meshach, and Abednego similar to the opening scene in Jonah's story?

2. Few in the Western world are faced with martyrdom like these guys were. Many can hide in a pseudo-Christian subculture without ever having to face consequences for following Christ. But those hiding places are dwindling. Is there anywhere in your life right now where following Christ puts you at risk? How?

Read Daniel 3:16-18

16 Shadrach, Meshach, and Abednego replied to the king, "Nebuchadnezzar, we don't need to give you an answer to this question. 17 If the God we serve exists, then He can rescue us from the furnace of blazing fire, and He can rescue us from the power of you, the king. 18 But even if He does not rescue us, we want you as king to know that we will not serve your gods or worship the gold statue you set up."

3. What words or phrases stand out to you in the reply these three guys gave to the king in the face of death? Why?

4. There's an old saying: Your true colors show when your feet are put to the fire. Jonah and the three men in Daniel 3 were all men of God. They all knew the same things about God. Why then did Jonah flee whereas the others stood firm?

5. What do you think keeps us from seeing and valuing God like the men in Daniel 3? Why do we drift into a Jonah-type relationship with God so often?

6. How would you articulate the promise of God we can cling to that gives us such joyful certainty in God's love and care for us? Feel free to share a favorite Bible verse.

Read Daniel 3:19-30

[19] Then Nebuchadnezzar was filled with rage, and the expression on his face changed toward Shadrach, Meshach, and Abednego. He gave orders to heat the furnace seven times more than was customary, [20] and he commanded some of the strongest soldiers in his army to tie up Shadrach, Meshach, and Abednego and throw them into the furnace of blazing fire. [23] And these three men, Shadrach, Meshach, and Abednego fell, bound, into the furnace of blazing fire. [24] Then King Nebuchadnezzar jumped up in alarm. He said to his advisers, "Didn't we throw three men, bound, into the fire?" "Yes, of course, Your Majesty," they replied to the king. [25] He exclaimed, "Look! I see four men, not tied, walking around in the fire unharmed; and the fourth looks like a son of the gods."

[26] Nebuchadnezzar then approached the door of the furnace of blazing fire and called: "Shadrach, Meshach, and Abednego, you servants of the Most High God—come out!" So Shadrach, Meshach, and Abednego came out of the fire. [27] When the satraps, prefects, governors, and the king's advisers gathered around, they saw that the fire had no effect on the bodies of these men: not a hair of their heads was singed, their robes were unaffected, and there was no smell of fire on them. [28] Nebuchadnezzar exclaimed, "Praise to the God of Shadrach, Meshach, and Abednego! He sent His angel and rescued His servants who trusted in Him. They violated the king's command and risked their lives rather than serve or worship any god except their own God. [29] Therefore I issue a decree that anyone of any people, nation, or language who says anything offensive against the God of Shadrach, Meshach, and Abednego will be torn limb from limb and his house made a garbage dump. For there is no other god who is able to deliver like this." [30] Then the king rewarded Shadrach, Meshach, and Abednego in the province of Babylon.

7. What are the similarities between the outcomes of Daniel 3 and Jonah 1?

8. How does this impact the way we view our love for and obedience to God?

Wrap-Up

REVIEW

1. Rebellion is simply saying "no" to God.
2. Our disobedience always affects others.
3. God sends storms into the lives of His people to wake them up from the slumber of sin.
4. The storms in our lives are not designed for retribution but for restoration.

CHALLENGE

In the box below, write out one achievable action step you can take this week in response to what you've discussed in this group.

PRAY TOGETHER

Notes

PERSONAL STUDY

The personal study portion of the weekly guide is designed to take you on a slow walk through the Book of Jonah. The hope in doing this is that you take time to consider what God is saying in these verses and what the implications are for your life. This week you will be in the opening chapter of Jonah. As you interact with the story, take note of what stands out to you and what God is teaching you. Use the questions at the end of each segment to help you consider the implications of this chapter for your life.

1. Jonah flees. Jonah 1:1-4

I (Spence) am a parent of three kids under the age of five. This new phase of life has thrown me headlong into the journey of molding a child's character. From little things like, "Son, you should not stand on your brother's head" to big things like teaching courage, honesty, and love, parenting is a wild ride. Just about any parent will tell you raising children is simultaneously one of the most exhausting and rewarding endeavors one can undertake.

It should come as no surprise to us that God's most common metaphor for teaching us how we relate to Him is the parent-child relationship. God loves and cares for each of us as a parent does a child. He knows what is best for us, and that's what He wants! He disciplines us to shape our character. We, like children, have a choice to make in our relationship with God. When His commands contradict our desires, we can choose to obey Him or our own desires. This is the dilemma so many longtime churchgoers have created in their minds. It presents itself as a choice to either do what I want to do, or do what God wants me to do.

This appears to be Jonah's dilemma here in the opening verses of chapter 1. Jonah's flight reveals his heart. His fears and hatred associated with Nineveh were more powerful to him than God is. So though he probably knew it wouldn't turn out well, he disobeyed and fled. Like a child, I often do the same thing. Though I know I cannot win this battle on my own, I just don't want to do what my Father is telling me to do. The only real solution to my disobedience isn't behavior modification, but belief transformation. Only when we begin to believe God is more valuable than anything else will we begin to live as if it is true. Like a loving parent, God is after our hearts, not our behavior.

Between you and God, what keeps you fighting against Him?

How would seeing obedience to God as delight rather than duty alter your relationship to Him?

In your opinion, what has to happen to reorient your relationship with Him?

Go to *www.lifeway.com/Jonah* for a video devotion with Spence Shelton.

2. God sends a storm of mercy. Jonah 1:4-11

"Then the Lord."

You have to wonder what Jonah's mentality was as he set out on that ship. As land faded away, did he have a glimmer of hope that maybe he had successfully fled from God? Regardless, by the time the storm on the sea showed up, Jonah knew what was happening. Despite his disobedience, God was not finished with Jonah. One thing you have to notice in these verses is the reaction of the sailors. We can assume they were not all rookies to storms on the sea. When it gets to the point where they give up on tactical maneuvering and start crying to their gods, you know it's a bad storm. The author (presumably Jonah) lets us know each man was crying out to "his god." He's setting up something for the readers here.

In an almost comical twist of irony, God redeemed Jonah's disobedience. Jonah ran from God because he didn't want to see God have mercy on Nineveh (see 4:2). Now God is even going to show mercy to the pagan sailors Jonah is using in his escape plan. When the lot fell to Jonah, the men finally questioned his identity, and in what sounds more like a confession than a mere answer, Jonah acknowledged he worshiped the one true God (1:9). In a panic, the sailors looked for an answer from Jonah. The seas were worsening.

The storm was a wake-up call for Jonah. Literally. It wasn't punishment; it was mercy. In the middle of a storm on the ocean, Jonah finally came clean about his flight. He was out of places to run. He'd gone down to Joppa, down to the dock, and down into the ship's lowest level. The story of Adam echoes in Jonah's hiding. This is everyone's story. We run from God, reject His Word, and follow empty escape plans filled with false promises of fulfillment. While often painfully hard to perceive in the moment, whatever "storm" God uses to draw us back to Himself is nothing short of mercy. While we don't want the storm, we should worship a God willing to save us through it. Not all storms are sent by God for such purposes, but God can bring great redemption through any storm.

What storms are going on in your life right now? Could any
of these be places where God is trying to get your attention?

Jonah's confession in verse 9 is a simple, powerful admission
of his own futility. How does his confession of who God
is help you process your own life situations right now?

3. God saves the sailors, God saves Jonah. Jonah 1:12-17

"Pick me up and throw me into the sea."

What Jonah? Throw you in? Do you see what's going on? I've always had trouble with Jonah's request here. Couldn't Jonah have just repented and asked God to stop everything? Why did he need to go overboard? But Jonah's story is part of a bigger story, a story of God's plan to reconcile people of all nations to Himself. The story of Jonah is not really about Jonah. It's about a God who loves His rebellious children and is pursuing them to bring them back to Himself. That's the story of Scripture. From Genesis 3, God is pursuing and redeeming His people.

In Jonah's case, the storm is not just a wake-up call to Jonah. It's a wake-up call to the sailors. In a scene that feels similar to Elijah on mount Carmel, the sailors' gods have no power. Only Yahweh, the one true God, has the power to save them. So in compliance to a rather absurd request, the sailors toss Jonah into the sea, and then verse 15 tells us the storm stopped raging. God showed His power, and the sailors' vows let us know in that moment they came to worship the one true God. God used Jonah, even in his disobedience, to weave more souls into His great salvation story.

But God was not done yet. Verse 17 tells us God saved Jonah as well. God wasn't finished using Jonah to save people, and so He saved Jonah. This is a major point. No one, not even the castaway hurled into the sea, is too far gone for God to save. This is where we take hope. Our God is not One to give up on us. He pursues us, reconciles us, and even when we don't see how, He make us ministers of reconciliation to others. God uses people to bring His message of hope to other people. And the message is the same. Our God is the one true God, and He saves.

Who in your circle of influence may God
be using you to tell His story to?

How does the realization that your story is about
God and others, not just you, change how you
perceive your life situation right now?

Week 2

THE FUTILITY OF LIFE
WITHOUT GOD

INTRODUCTION

"Religion is a crutch." I heard this more times than I can remember during four years of undergraduate studies at my beloved university. I heard it from classmates, roommates, and professors alike. To many, religion was simply something weaker people needed to help them deal with life when bad times came along. And once the storm was weathered, you could put God back on the shelf.

Often I found myself agreeing with them. I would just go to God when exams hit or when my girlfriend and I had a fight. I was really just using God to help me get back on my feet and then continuing on with my plan. God and I were on good terms as long as those things were in order. But like Jonah, God brought me to a place where I realized I couldn't play the "I heart God" game while still having areas where I was using Him. My friends were right, God as a crutch was hypocrisy. Like Jonah, I learned God is a stretcher, not a crutch. You do not lean on a stretcher; you put your entire weight on it.

Jonah's rich prayer in chapter 2 reveals the mind of a man who finally understood that God alone could rescue him. God took Jonah to a place where he was completely without hope apart from God. And here in that place Jonah's prayer gives us a litmus test for our own souls. Jonah is desperate. He is literally and figuratively at the lowest point of his life. And here, in the disgusting belly of a fish, a prayer that rivals the best of the psalms is offered. The castaway surrenders.

Warm-Up

1. Okay, not a fun one but did you ever not get something you really put effort and hope into getting? (For example, not make a team, not get a promotion you thought you were getting, or get turned down for a date?) What did that feel like?

2. Why do you think those moments linger with us throughout life?

Video Setup

In this video J.D. is going to look into the first half of Jonah's prayer in chapter 2. We are going to see what it took for Jonah to come to a place where he could finally obey God.

Play Video 2: "Futility."

Video Guide

The first major concept in Jonah's prayer of repentance is the futility of
_____ _____ _____.

Repentance always begins in a note of _____.

Better to be united with God even in the belly of a fish than on dry land
without Him! The real pit is _____ _____ _____, not
a particular circumstance.

The second major realization in Jonah's prayer is the emptiness
of _____.

When you turn to an idol, you _____ the grace that could be yours.

The third major realization in Jonah's prayer is _____ belongs
to the Lord.

Seeing that Jesus was cast into the _____ ____ ____ _____ for
us gives us the motivation for the new kind of obedience.

Video Feedback

Here is a good chance for you to tell your own story about how God
has revealed to you the emptiness of life without Him. If you are now a
Christian, what did this faith journey look like in your life?

If you have not yet come to faith, describe your spiritual journey to this
point or perhaps share what you have seen in someone else's life that has
made the Christian walk attractive to you.

If you missed this session, you can download the
video teaching from *www.lifeway.com/Jonah*

Group Discussion

ISAIAH 44:6-20

The prayer of the prophet Jonah praises the sovereign grace of God as the only means of salvation for him. He realizes to depend upon anything else is idolatry, and it will get him nowhere. The knowledge of the emptiness of idols is of course not unique to Jonah. Isaiah is another prophet who God raised up to speak His Word to His people and Isaiah spent much of his time urging Israel away from idolatry.

The Book of Isaiah is one of the longest in the Bible and is almost entirely filled with God's admonitions to His people. While some passages are a little complex at first read, others are straightforward and almost satirical in tone. Isaiah 44:6-20 is one of the plainest explanations of idolatry we will find anywhere in the Bible. Considering this passage will help you fully understand the futility of Jonah's flight, the emptiness of idols, and his confession that salvation belongs to the Lord.

Read Isaiah 44:6-8

---

6 This is what the Lord, the King of Israel and
its Redeemer, the Lord of Hosts, says:
I am the first and I am the last.
There is no God but Me.
7 Who, like Me, can announce the future?
Let him say so and make a case before Me,
since I have established an ancient people.
Let these gods declare the coming things,
and what will take place.
8 Do not be startled or afraid.
Have I not told you and declared it long ago?
You are my witnesses!
Is there any God but Me?
There is no other Rock; I do not know any.
and their minds so they cannot understand.

1. Focus in on Isaiah 44:6-8. Summarize the message of these verses into one short thought.

2. This is perhaps the most central teaching of Scripture. Jonah's prayer acknowledges God's sovereignty over creation. Yet it took Jonah three days in a fish belly to get to this point. Why is such a simple teaching repeated so often so hard for us to live by?

Read Isaiah 44:9-20

9 All who make idols are nothing,
and what they treasure does not profit.
Their witnesses do not see or know anything,
so they will be put to shame.
10 Who makes a god or casts a metal image
for no profit?
11 Look, all its worshipers will be put to shame,
and the craftsmen are humans.
They all will assemble and stand;
they all will be startled and put to shame.
12 The ironworker labors over the coals,
shapes the idol with hammers,
and works it with his strong arm.
Also he grows hungry and his strength fails;
he doesn't drink water and is faint.
13 The woodworker stretches out a measuring line,
he outlines it with a stylus;
he shapes it with chisels
and outlines it with a compass.

He makes it according to a human likeness,
like a beautiful person,
to dwell in a temple.
14 He cuts down cedars for his use,
or he takes a cypress or an oak.
He lets it grow strong among the trees of the forest.
He plants a laurel, and the rain makes it grow.
15 It serves as fuel for man.
He takes some of it and warms himself;
also he kindles a fire and bakes bread;
he even makes it into a god and worships it;
he makes an idol from it and bows down to it.
16 He burns half of it in a fire,
and he roasts meat on that half.
He eats the roast and is satisfied.
He warms himself and says, "Ah!
I am warm, I see the blaze."
17 He makes a god or his idol with the rest of it.
He bows down to it and worships;
He prays to it, "Save me, for you are my god."
18 Such people do not comprehend
and cannot understand,
for He has shut their eyes so they cannot see,
19 No one reflects,
no one has the perception or insight to say,
"I burned half of it in the fire,
I also baked bread on its coals,
I roasted meat and ate.
I will make something detestable with the rest of it,
and I will bow down to a block of wood."
20 He feeds on ashes.
His deceived mind has led him astray,
and he cannot deliver himself,
or say, "Isn't there a lie in my right hand?"

3. Now look at verses 9-20, specifically the illustrations of the carpenter and the ironsmith. In these illustrations, what do you think the characters and their crafts represent?

4. Relying on verses 17-20 to guide you, what is the simple irony God is communicating in these illustrations?

5. What danger are both Isaiah and Jonah saying comes with idol worship?

6. Ok, time to transition out of the illustrations and into real life. For most of us, we aren't bowing down to blocks of wood. But we do sacrifice time, money, and energy to the things we value. What are common idols among your circles of friends and family?

7. How do verses 21-23 of Isaiah 44 and verses 6-9 of Jonah 2 call you back from times of idol worship?

Wrap-Up

REVIEW

1. Life is futile without God.
2. Repentance always begins in a note of despair.
3. When you turn to an idol, you forfeit the grace that could be yours.
4. Salvation belongs to the Lord.

CHALLENGE

In the box below, write out one achievable action step you can take this week in response to what you've discussed in this group.

PRAY TOGETHER

Notes

PERSONAL STUDY

The personal study portion of the weekly guide is designed to take you on a slow walk through the Book of Jonah. The hope in doing this is you take time to consider what God is saying in these verses and what the implications are for your life. This week you will walk through the first part of Jonah's prayer in chapter 2. Take time to respond to the questions and write down anything you think God is trying to tell you through these words of Scripture.

1. In the belly of a fish. Jonah 2:1-3

The beginning of the second chapter of Jonah is no pleasant scene. Jonah has been inside the digestive tract of a giant fish for three days. The imagery is almost too grotesque to put into words. Suffice it to say the author wants us to know Jonah is at his all-time low point. Notice that it still took Jonah three days to get to the point where he prayed this prayer. Important for the reader to notice is a transition in genre from narrative to poetry akin to the psalms. This allows the prayer to express vivid imagery and meaning. The opening verses deliver significant truths that Jonah is finally coming to terms with.

- God hears the cry for help. Even when Jonah is in *Sheol* God hears him. *Sheol* is a Hebrew term that is used to communicate the grave, or the lowest possible place in creation. Yet *Sheol* was not beyond God's range.

- God is in control. Even though the sailors cast Jonah overboard, Jonah acknowledged God's sovereignty. He acknowledged God's hand in sending him into the belly of the fish, even God's authority over the oceans. Jonah realized nothing that was happening was surprising to God or outside His control.

- God offers hope. Though Jonah was "driven away" (v. 4, ESV)from God's sight, he had a resolved hope that he would again be restored to

God. He would pray in the presence of God, which in effect means he would be reconciled to God.

These truths are central for us today. There is a God who is able and willing to save us, to restore us to Himself. Whether you find yourself in the belly of a proverbial fish right now, or just walking through a monotonous season of life, God is here and He hears you.

What does your relationship with God look like right now? Does your prayer life reflect a belief in God's ability and willingness to save you?

Write down the biggest obstacle you have to believing God will help you. Then acknowledge that obstacle to God and ask for His help. Rest in the promise that on the cross God has proven He is willing and able to meet your deepest needs.

Go to *www.lifeway.com/Jonah* for a video devotion with Spence Shelton.

2. Rescued from the pit. Jonah 2:4-6

This prayer of Jonah has a chiastic structure to it. A chiasm is a classic Hebrew linguistic structure, often employed in the psalms, designed to communicate meaning not just in the words but in the ordering of the words as well. The chiasm in this prayer is found in the directional language of Jonah. The prayer reaches a climax in verse 6 where Jonah has been going further and further down until the point where we now find him at death's door. It seems Jonah borrowed from a few psalms in building this prayer, but verses 5 and 6 appear to be uniquely his. You can almost feel death wrapping its arms around his dying body. This is where the musical score would probably go silent because it looks like no hope is left. Jonah is finished "forever." Then of course the turning point. There in verse 6 rest the great words that make up the anthem of every Christian: "Yet you brought up my life from the pit, O LORD my God" (ESV).

The only way we can truly comprehend salvation is to understand our dilemma without Christ. As Ephesians 2 says, we were all dead in our sins. Only the sinner who understands the magnitude of his sin can cry out to God, like Jonah, to save his life. Each of us must travel Jonah's path to the pit. We must come to a place where we realize life without Christ is nothing but death. And the only hope we have is Christ coming to save us. Then and only then can we exercise true repentance and experience the unmerited favor of God found in the blood of Christ.

If you are a Christian, think back to when you
decided to follow Christ. How did you come to
realize the dangers of life apart from Christ? Who
helped you take the step to follow Christ?

We never grow beyond this message of salvation,
only deeper into it. In what ways does this
message give you a fresh hope today?

3. Remember the Lord. Jonah 2:7

Prayer is an important spiritual discipline in the life of Christ followers. Here in verse 7 of Jonah's prayer, Jonah experiences prayer not merely as a discipline, but as his only hope. This is the cry of the man whose "life was fainting away" (ESV). Jonah's words represent the words of every man or woman who has truly come to a place where they are utterly hopeless. Jonah's words give hope to every one of us. First, he "remembered the LORD." We know of course from earlier in the prayer that the Lord remembered him. This is never in question, for the Lord had been pursuing Jonah since his first step toward Joppa. But now Jonah remembered God. It is not as if Jonah had forgotten that God exists. He was very aware at that point the Lord is real and present. What brings hope to the reader here is that Jonah remembers the Lord saves. Even when life is fading away, Jonah could turn to the Lord and know his prayer would reach God's "holy temple" (ESV).

The temple is an important symbol in biblical literature. The temple represents the dwelling place of God. Whether it was the portable tabernacle of Moses' day, or the grand temple of Solomon, it was always associated with the presence of God. Jonah believes his prayer from the darkest depths will reach the very throne of heaven. And the God who hears it is the One who is able and willing to save those who repent and turn to Him.

When it seems the Lord is silent and distant while everything is crashing in on you, Jonah reminds us the Lord is very near. This is the truth of Hebrews 4:16: "Let us approach the throne of grace with boldness, so that we may receive mercy and find grace to help us at the proper time." The gospel says God has not forgotten you. He remembered you on the cross when He provided for you the very thing you needed most. In this love you find not silence but a chorus of grace declaring love over you. God is near. The more you remember His mercy in Christ, the more you realize His desire to care for you as His child.

Would you characterize your recent interaction
with God as distant or intimate? Why?

How does remembering the gospel
give you confidence in prayer?

Pray and ask God to give you a felt sense of
His presence through His Holy Spirit.

Week 3

SALVATION BELONGS
TO THE LORD

INTRODUCTION

Every year the Gallup organization surveys Americans to find out who they most admire in the world. The results list the top 10 men and top 10 women, usually including people in government, religious leaders, and philanthropists. While the list varies from year to year, Billy Graham has finished in the top 10 a record-breaking 55 years, 49 in a row including another 4th place finish in 2011. The closest to him is Queen Elizabeth II of England with 44 years in the top 10.[1]

While admired for so many years, Rev. Graham's contribution to the world is in one sense very narrow compared to the other names on the list. He has never led a country or built a revolutionary company. He did of course lead a large organization, but that organization had one simple agenda: to share this simple message that salvation belongs to the Lord. Something about this message captivated Americans. Through the years, stadiums have filled up night after night to hear Rev. Graham preach this message.

The message is not new with Rev. Graham. It is the most important, influential message in human history and we each have to deal with it. This is the same message our prophet Jonah gives at the end of his prayer in chapter 2. Salvation belongs to the Lord. This message confronted Jonah, the pagan sailors, Nineveh, and it confronts you and me today. Salvation belongs to the Lord.

GROUP STUDY

Warm-Up

1. Who has been the most influential
person to your faith? Why?

2. What from your personal study of Jonah
has impacted you most up to this point?

Video Setup

In this session J.D. is going to explain the end of Jonah's prayer, his message of salvation, and its implications for us.

Play Video 3: "Salvation."

Video Guide

Identify and describe the two ways J.D. says you have to read the Book of Jonah:

1.

2.

All that the _____ Jonah did wrong, Jesus the _____ did right.

Knowing that you might get swallowed by a fish if you disobey might change your _____, but knowing Jesus was swallowed by death in your place will change your _____.

God isn't just after obedience; He's after a _____ _____ _____ of obedience, an obedience that grows from _____, an obedience fueled by _____.

Being put in the belly of a whale can _____ your obedience; seeing Jesus went into the real belly of the whale is what creates _____ in your heart.

Video Feedback

How is Jesus like Jonah? How is He different?

Discuss the questions that J.D. asked at the end of the video. Which question was most relevant for you? Feel free to discuss your spiritual journey together.

If you missed this session, you can download the video teaching from *www.lifeway.com/Jonah*

Group Discussion

ACTS 4:5-22

Jonah's message of salvation is certainly not confined to the Book of Jonah. It is the central message of the Bible. It runs like a thick thread through all 66 books, tying them together regardless of genre or date of authorship. The Book of Acts shows the church picking up this same message. In Acts 4:5-22 the apostle Peter is asked by the local authorities, the Sadducees, to explain by what power or name he healed a lame beggar (Acts 3:1-11). The setting is the day after Peter and John had spent a night in jail for preaching their message of salvation. In Peter's response to this interrogation there rings a familiar tone of humble confidence reminiscent of Jonah's prayer in Jonah 2. Jonah was humbled by being in the belly of a fish, yet confident God was powerful and gracious enough to rescue him. Peter was humble enough to quickly give credit for any miracle to the name of Jesus, and was confident in Christ's sovereignty enough to speak boldly to these authorities knowing it may cost him his life. Peter's message of salvation gives New Testament clarity to Jonah's Old Testament proclamation in Jonah 2.

Read Acts 4:5-22.

> [5] The next day, their rulers, elders, and scribes assembled in Jerusalem [6] with Annas the high priest, Caiaphas, John and Alexander, and all the members of the high-priestly family.
> [7] After they had Peter and John stand before them, they asked the question: "By what power or in what name have you done this?"
> [8] Then Peter was filled with the Holy Spirit and said to them, "Rulers of the people and elders: [9] If we are being examined today about a good deed done to a disabled man—by what means he was healed—[10] let it be known to all of you and to all the people of Israel, that by the name of Jesus Christ the Nazarene—whom you crucified and whom God raised from the dead—by Him this man is standing here before you healthy. [11] This Jesus is the stone rejected by you builders, which has become the cornerstone.
> [12] There is salvation in no one else, for there is no other name under heaven given to people, and we must be saved by it."

[13] When they observed the boldness of Peter and John and realized that they were uneducated and untrained men, they were amazed and recognized that they had been with Jesus. [14] And since they saw the man who had been healed standing with them, they had nothing to say in response.

[15] After they had ordered them to leave the Sanhedrin, they conferred among themselves, [16] saying, "What should we do with these men? For an obvious sign, evident to all who live in Jerusalem, has been done through them, and we cannot deny it! [17] However, so this does not spread any further among the people, let's threaten them against speaking to anyone in this name again." [18] So they called for them and ordered them not to preach or teach at all in the name of Jesus.

[19] But Peter and John answered them, "Whether it's right in the sight of God for us to listen to you rather than to God, you decide; [20] for we are unable to stop speaking about what we have seen and heard."

[21] After threatening them further, they released them. They found no way to punish them, because the people were all giving glory to God over what had been done; [22] for this sign of healing had been performed on a man over [40] years old.

1. Focus first on Acts 4:5-12. What claims does Peter make about Jesus?

2. Peter switches from talking about healing
to talking about salvation. What connection is
Peter making that exists between healing and
salvation? Why should this matter for us?

3. What parallels do you see between Jonah's prayer
in Jonah 2 and Peter's message in Acts 4? What
differences do you see and why are they significant?

4. At this point the message of salvation is clear ... sort of.
Where salvation comes from is clear, but how one receives
it is not. Using what you've learned up to this point,
explain how one receives the salvation offered in Christ.

5. Like the Sadducees, some people today get upset when they hear Christians proclaim the message that Jesus is the only means of salvation. What can we learn from Peter and John for how we engage those who may be hostile to the gospel?

6. Acts 4:19-20 gives the reader a quick look into the inner motivation of the people of the early church. Why are their words so important to a healthy perspective on the Christian life?

Wrap-Up

REVIEW

1. All that the prophet Jonah did wrong, Jesus the Messiah did right.

2. Lasting behavior change will occur not because of fear of circumstances but because of real heart change.

3. God isn't just after obedience; He's after a whole new kind of obedience, an obedience that grows from desire.

4. Seeing that Jesus went into the real belly of the whale is what creates desire in your heart.

CHALLENGE

In the box below, write out one achievable action step you can take this week in response to what you've discussed in this group.

PRAY TOGETHER

Notes

PERSONAL STUDY

The personal study portion of the weekly guide is designed to take you on a slow walk through the Book of Jonah. The hope in doing this is you take time to consider what God is saying in these verses and what the implications are for your life. This week you will only cover three verses, Jonah 2:8-10. These are some of the richest words in all of Jonah, so take time to meditate and reflect on them. You may want to consider memorizing them.

1. The deception of your idols. Jonah 2:8

Jonah has just remembered the Lord (v. 7) and is, at this moment, thinking clearly. His words, though brief, carry that God-breathed power that separates Scripture from anything else put to paper. To realize only the Lord can save him means to realize nothing else can save him, not even himself. But let's not be quick to assume Jonah's realization is just about himself. It's more likely this is one of those places where Jonah, writing after the actual events, is giving a clear indictment of all Israel. The imagery of the language is important to grasp alongside the teaching point. To "cling" is to hold fast to something, which implies present active, mental, and physical energy. You cannot cling to something you aren't paying a good amount of attention to. And usually you cling to something when you need it to help you in some way. Jonah is reminding us that depending on anything other than God is like trying to climb a rope that is not attached to anything. The more you tug on it, the more rope you get until eventually as the saying goes, you are at the end of your rope. Jonah is calling Israel to cling again to the One who has the power to save, the same One who had saved them and whom they had forsaken at some point along the way.

Spouses, careers, sports, popularity, academics, are all ropes with no attachment on the other end. They are good things and often gifts from God, but worthless as saviors to cling to. So Jonah reminds us, do not forsake faithful love. Do not forsake the only One who will save when you cling to Him. This is the gospel of Jonah. Only Christ saves, so cling to Him.

What in your life are you holding onto too tightly right now? This is something you should pray through and ask God to reveal to you.

In the gospel we find the "faithful love" Jonah talked about. If you are a Christian, reflect on how you've experienced that love in Christ.

If you are not a Christian, what is keeping you from putting your faith in Christ?

Go to *www.lifeway.com/Jonah* for a video devotion with Spence Shelton.

2. *Salvation belongs to the Lord. Jonah 2:9*

This is the headline verse in Jonah. This confession of Jonah is the confession of every prophet, of Christ, and of every man and woman who chooses to follow Christ.

The word for "salvation" here is from the Hebrew word transliterated as *yesua*. Names like Hosea, Joshua, Isaiah, and most notably Jesus all derive from this same Hebrew word. This is the central call of Scripture. Since the fall man has needed saving. And that saving comes from one place only: the Lord. When Jonah says he will sacrifice to God with "the voice of thanksgiving" he is saying that he will worship the Lord instead of the idols worshiped by the foolish. He is declaring his allegiance to the Lord. Every word here matters. Salvation is the deepest need of the human race. Our sin has separated us from God and put a death sentence on each of us. We are each now looking at death with no power to escape it. We need to be rescued.

This salvation belongs to someone. It has an owner, a giver. It is not abstract nor is it a set of rules to follow; it is the property of Someone. We cannot buy it, earn it, or steal it. It must be given. Salvation belongs to the Lord. The God of the universe owns the rights to our salvation. It is His to give. When God sent Christ to die for the sins of mankind, He extended this salvation to all men. Through Christ, God offers redemption and restoration to all men. The death sentence facing you was paid by the only One who could give you this salvation, and in place of the death you deserved He offers you life. This is what the apostle Paul was referring to when he said in Romans 5:18, "As through one trespass there is condemnation for everyone, so also through one righteous act there is life-giving justification for everyone." Salvation belongs to the Lord and has been given by Him to us. Our lives are indicators of how we respond to that simple, most profound reality.

Do you believe salvation belongs to the Lord? If
not, where do you think it comes from?

How have you personally experienced this
truth? From what has God saved you?

How does your life reflect that you are living
in response to this reality? How could it?

3. Dry land. Jonah 2:10

Here at the end of Jonah 2 we find a simple, image-rich statement transitioning us back from Jonah's poetic interlude into the narration of the story. This verse is the physical result of Jonah's confession that salvation belongs to the Lord. It should not surprise us the author includes the anecdotal note that the Lord spoke to the fish. The fish didn't decide to expel Jonah from his belly. No, God saw fit to get Jonah back in the game so He spoke to the fish. Jonah is giving the same color commentary he gave in verse 3 when talking about God's ownership of the seas. The sea, storm, the fish, and everything else in creation are at the Lord's command. This theme is not unique to Jonah. Old Testament narrative texts tell of God's control over creation, and the poetic texts praise Him because of it. In God's omnipotence, He sets Jonah onto dry land.

This scene—a giant fish vomiting a living human onto the beach—is both grotesque and to most guys, pretty awesome. There lies Jonah, body in the sand covered in the stench of three-day-old fish guts. I can imagine the words Jonah spoke lying there that didn't make it into the final draft of this book by God's choice. But one thing is for sure; this is God's deliverance. By no means is this a sweet, fairytale deliverance, but it is deliverance nonetheless. Jonah lifts his eyes to see light for the first time in days. His God has saved him, and will be setting him back on the course He has for him.

Now that you've come to the end of Jonah's prayer, what has God taught you through it?

How does God's control over creation help you relate to Him as Savior?

Week 4

THE MAKING OF
A WITNESS

INTRODUCTION

As heir to the Borden Dairy estate, William Borden was already a millionaire when he graduated high school in 1904. His graduation present from his parents was a trip around the world. As the 16-year-old Borden traveled through Asia, the Middle East, and Europe, he felt a growing burden for the world's hurting people. Finally, he wrote home to say, "I'm going to give my life to prepare for the mission field." One friend expressed surprise that he was "throwing himself away as a missionary." In response, Borden wrote two words in the back of his Bible: "No reserves." Borden's missionary call narrowed to the Muslim Kansu people in China. Once that goal was in sight, Borden never wavered.

Upon graduating from Yale, Borden turned down multiple high-paying job offers. In his Bible, he wrote two more words: "No retreats." Borden went on to graduate work at Princeton Seminary in New Jersey. When he finished his studies at Princeton, he sailed for China. Because he was hoping to work with Muslims, he stopped first in Egypt to study Arabic. While there, he contracted spinal meningitis. Within a month, 25-year-old William Borden was dead.

When news of Borden's death was cabled back to the U.S., nearly every American newspaper carried the story: "A wave of sorrow went round the world ... Borden not only gave away his wealth, but himself, in a way so joyous and natural that it seemed a privilege rather than a sacrifice," wrote Mary Taylor in her introduction to his biography.[2]

Does Borden's untimely death render his life a waste? Not in God's plan. Prior to his death, Borden wrote two more words in his Bible. Underneath the words "No reserves" and "No retreats," he had written "No regrets."

GROUP STUDY

Warm-Up

1. Share a time when you were given a second chance
at something. Why did you take the second chance?

2. When you think of a missionary or witness,
what type of person comes to mind? Why?

Video Set-up

In this session J.D. will look at Jonah's journey to Nineveh where he
preached God's Word and Nineveh responded. In Jonah we will see what
is and what is not the responsibility of a witness.

Play Video 4: "Witness."

Video Guide

God blesses us to be a _____ to others.

Becoming an effective witness requires that you know two things:

1. _____ belongs to the Lord (Jonah 2:9).

We're not dealing with skeptics who need to be _____; we are dealing with _____ people who need to be _____ to life.

2. _____ comes only by hearing (Romans 10:17).

The Word cannot do its work where people haven't _____ it.

Knowing this should lead us to two things:

1. Get people in the presence of the _____ _____ _____.

2. _____ like crazy.

Video Feedback

How do you respond to J.D.'s question, "If God answered right now, in one fell swoop, every prayer you prayed last week, would anybody new be in the kingdom?" Discuss.

How does knowing salvation belongs to the Lord influence how you view sharing Christ with others?

 If you missed this session, you can download the video teaching from *www.lifeway.com/Jonah*

Group Discussion

2 CORINTHIANS 5:11-21 AND A GOSPEL EXERCISE

The apostle Paul held tight to a perspective on the death and resurrection of Christ that compelled him to live a singularly motivated life seeking the glory of God. This passage ties the awe Paul felt over the grace of God to his unparalleled zeal for preaching the gospel to those who hadn't heard it yet. Paul said he was compelled by the love of Christ in such a way that he could live for himself any longer but for Christ, the One who died and then was raised. Like Jonah, Paul was simply the mouthpiece of God's working in the world. It is our job to preach, and God's job to appeal through us.

Read 2 Corinthians 5:11-21

¹¹ Therefore, knowing the fear of the Lord, we persuade others. But what we are is known to God, and I hope it is known also to your conscience. ¹² We are not commending ourselves to you again but giving you cause to boast about us, so that you may be able to answer those who boast about outward appearance and not about what is in the heart. ¹³ For if we are beside ourselves, it is for God; if we are in our right mind, it is for you. ¹⁴ For the love of Christ controls us, because we have concluded this: that one has died for all, therefore all have died; ¹⁵ and he died for all, that those who live might no longer live for themselves but for him who for their sake died and was raised.¹⁶ From now on, therefore, we regard no one according to the flesh. Even though we once regarded Christ according to the flesh, we regard him thus no longer. ¹⁷ Therefore, if anyone is in Christ, he is a new creation. The old has passed away; behold, the new has come. ¹⁸ All this is from God, who through Christ reconciled us to himself and gave us the ministry of reconciliation; ¹⁹ that is, in Christ God was reconciling the world to himself, not counting their trespasses against them, and entrusting to us the message of reconciliation. ²⁰ Therefore, we are ambassadors for Christ, God making his appeal through us. We implore you on behalf of Christ, be reconciled to God. ²¹ For our sake he made him to be sin who knew no sin, so that in him we might become the righteousness of God.

What Jonah and Paul both teach us is that there is power in the Word of God when preached. The power is not in either of these men, but in the living and active Word of God. God chose people to be His Plan A to tell other people His Word. When we engage in preaching God's message, God Himself is empowering our words in the ears of the hearer. Jonah, Paul, and all Christians are thus ministers of reconciliation. We do not have the power to reconcile, but the love of Christ compels us to make visible the reconciliation God offers.

1. If you are a Christian, do you remember where you were when you decided to follow Christ? What do you recall about the moment? What do you recall about the message?

2. A recent study by LifeWay Research found that 80% of regular church attenders believe it is their responsibility to share the gospel, but 61% of them have not done so in the last six months.[3] We seem more like Jonah than Paul. We know we are supposed to share Christ, but we don't do it. What is missing?

3. Who are the people in your circle of influence who may have never clearly heard this message of salvation? List their names here and ask the group to pray for them.

4. What is a feasible next step you can take to share the message of salvation with them?

Group Exercise

At this point, divide into smaller groupings of two or three. In these groups, practice sharing the gospel message with one another. Do not worry if it seems awkward at first. Beyond the awkwardness is the joy of hearing and speaking the gospel to one another.

NOTE: Refer to the Gospel Presentation guide in the back of this workbook for help you if you aren't sure where to begin.

5. In the exercise, what did you find easiest about sharing the gospel? What was most difficult?

Wrap-Up

REVIEW

1. God blesses us to be a blessing to others.

2. Becoming an effective witness requires that you understand two things: salvation belongs to the Lord and faith comes only by hearing.

3. The Word cannot do its work where people haven't heard it.

4. Our objective is to get people in the presence of the Word of God.

CHALLENGE

In the box below, write out one achievable action step you can take this week in response to what you've discussed in this group.

PRAY TOGETHER

Notes

PERSONAL STUDY

The personal study portion of the weekly guide is designed to take you on a slow walk through the Book of Jonah. The hope in doing this is you take time to consider what God is saying in these verses and what the implications are for your life. This week you will cover Jonah 3. As you walk through Jonah's journey into Nineveh, take time to write some notes down and meditate on what God is saying to you.

1. A second chance. Jonah 3:1-5

"Then the word of the LORD came to Jonah the second time" (v. 1). How many Christians can relate to this moment in Jonah's life? Can you? The moment where God's persistent grace comes again, calling to you after you thought you'd driven Him away. Now you look back and thank God for persisting through your stubbornness and giving you another chance to surrender your weary fight and submit to Him as Lord. For Jonah, the call didn't change. God didn't qualify it or remind Jonah of his past failure. He simply gave him the same call, verbatim, to go preach to Nineveh. The God of grace doesn't hold your rebellion over your head. The gospel simply calls you to obedience in Christ.

Jonah's sermon to Nineveh is one you do not hear modeled often. There is no call for repentance or beautiful explanation of God's grace. His message consists of seven words that together make up a warning of God's impending destruction of Nineveh. From what we know of the rest of Jonah's story, you can almost imagine a wild-eyed Jonah walking deep through enemy territory declaring destruction. He couldn't run; he'd already tried that. The only obvious outcome of him being here, let alone preaching, is his imminent death. So at this point, what did he have to lose? He held nothing back and preached exactly what God told him to preach in chapter 1. What happened next is the result of the simple, profound power of God on display: Nineveh believed in God. What a redemption story. As one author said it "The salvation of one Hebrew sinner is intended to produce the salvation of many Ninevite sinners."[4] The worst of the worst, the Ninevites, are saved on the spot following a seven-word sermon. God is showing again here that salvation belongs to Him and no one else.

How have you experienced God's persistent grace in your life? Any time in particular you can recount?

What is God calling you toward that you have been resisting Him in? What is keeping you from obeying this time?

Go to *www.lifeway.com/Jonah* for a video devotion with Spence Shelton.

2. Nineveh repents. Jonah 3:6-9

The "word" in verse six is most likely the Word of the Lord, the sermon Jonah preached walking through Nineveh. The king's response is an echo of Jonah 1:6 (and v. 14) where the pagan sailors cry out for salvation from the judgment of God saying, "Perhaps the god will give a thought to us, that we may not perish" (ESV). The irony cannot go unnoticed in Jonah. Wherever this rebellious prophet went, God brought salvation to the people around him. Many obedient prophets in the Old Testament never got to see the repentance of their hearers the way Jonah did. God has ensured in the story of Jonah that we can only attribute the salvation of the sailors and the people of Nineveh to God. There is simply no other explanation. Salvation belongs to the Lord.

We are not sure who the "king" is (though most likely a part of the Assyrian empire), but his word is clearly law. Do not overlook what appear to be superfluous details in verse 6. The king got off of his throne and took off his royal robes. Jonah is showing us the humbling of the pagan king, and subsequently a pagan nation, before God. There is no guarantee God will relent at this point, but the king fell to the ground putting himself and his nation at the mercy of God. Jonah in this narrative is a representative of the people of Israel. Here God is indicting Israel for its rebellious heart toward a God to whom even its worst enemies are bowing down and worshiping. Israel was the nation God had already brought salvation to, yet so often they forgot their God and rebelled against His Word. That is Jonah, and that is you and me. Let the apparent absurdity of Jonah's stubborn fight against God be a warning to you and me to constantly guard our hearts and minds from hardening to the voice of the very God who saved us.

God saved one of the most corrupted nations in human history when He saved Nineveh. Who in your life are you convinced is too far gone? That represents a belief that salvation belongs to you and not to the Lord. Confess that to God, repent, and ask God to save those people.

Where in your life are you trying to muffle the voice of God? Pray for God to keep you from becoming hardened to His saving grace and ask for help from His Spirit to obey His Word.

3. *God spares Nineveh. Jonah 3:10*

This is one of those moments in Scripture that can get swept into debates on God's sovereignty and robbed of its own beauty and message to the reader in the context of the narrative. The text is straightforward and repetitive, a sign the author is trying to drive home his point. It's clear from the task God gave Jonah in Jonah 2:1 that God wanted to spare Nineveh. Why else would He send someone to preach? If God wanted to wipe Nineveh off the map He could have done so. The tragic story of Sodom and Gomorrah teaches us this. We see something different here. In Nineveh we see in action the mercy of God Peter spoke of saying the Lord "is patient with you, not wanting any to perish but all to come to repentance" (2 Peter 3:9). God's patience with Nineveh is displayed by sending Jonah to them. His mercy is clear in verse 10 where the author very clearly tells us God spared Nineveh in response to their repentance. The Hebrew word for God's change of mind is literally "repentance." Just as Nineveh turned from their ways, so God turned from His plans to destroy them.

As a Bible student, alarm bells should be going off here. This is the great theme of the Bible. Mankind rebels against God, deserving punishment for their sin. And though God could justly punish, He instead shows mercy. Dead in our sin, God sends a Savior to bring us back from death and reconciles us to Himself. Reconciliation to God the Father is our deepest need. On the cross Jesus paid the debt we owed for our sin so that we might be spared the judgment owed to us. That is why John says "Love consists in this: not that we loved God, but that He loved us and sent His Son to be the propitiation for our sins" (1 John 4:10). In this narrative of Jonah, we are to see in Nineveh our own reflection: a people deserving death for our rebellion. Like Nineveh, we should repent and thank God He spared us in Christ.

If you are a Christian, recall when you began following Christ. How did God bring you to a place of repentance and belief like He did for Nineveh?

What do you sense God is teaching you about Himself through this chapter of Jonah?

Week 5

THE PROBLEM
WITH RELIGION

INTRODUCTION

In January of 2009 several people in northern Japan fell ill after eating blowfish that was prepared improperly by a chef not licensed to prepare the poisonous fish. Blowfish poison is significantly more toxic than potassium cyanide and can cause death within an hour and a half of ingestion. The diners surely assumed that such a decent-looking restaurant would have a proper license for cooking "fugu," the Japanese term for blowfish. In this case, their ignorance to the circumstances around them nearly cost them their lives.[5]

I (Spence) often teach various groups about the value and practice of community in the Christian life. One of the principles I try to incorporate every time is that we all have blind spots in our spiritual life that we need others pointing out to us before they do real damage to us. A blind spot could be a relationship that is reaching an unhealthy place. It could be overworking to compensate for issues at home. True community breaks through sin's deception to bring gospel truth to bear on these problems that we are often ignorant of. Sometimes we are ignorant of their existence in our lives. Other times we acknowledge their presence but are ignorant of their destructive power. In this session Jonah's ignorance to the grace of God goes on trial as Jonah's anger puts him in the middle of a debate with God.

GROUP STUDY

Warm-Up

1. Share about a time when you felt like God didn't respond to a situation the way you wanted or asked Him to. How did you feel at the time? How do you feel now?

2. Share about a time when you found yourself after the fact saying, "If I'd only known …"

Video Setup

In this session J.D. will look at the first half of the fourth and final chapter in the Book of Jonah. Here we will see how Jonah's idolatry and his ignorance created enmity between him and God. Again we will see God's patience and grace at work.

Play Video 5: "Religion."

Video Guide

An idol is the one thing that has to be part of your _____ in order for life to be worth living.

Jonah's two-fold disease:

1. Jonah is an _____.

2. Jonah is _____.

When you see yourself as a recipient of great grace, then God's _____ becomes His most precious attribute to you, and you want to be like Him.

A person who understands _____ _____ in their life is continually amazed by how much of it they have in their life.

You are _____ a sinner to God and only _____ someone who is sinned against.

A spirit of _____ and a lack of _____ is the indication you are out of touch with the grace of God in your own life.

Video Feedback

How was Jonah's sin worse than Nineveh's? Did this convict you in any way personally? Discuss.

J.D. said to "see yourself as sinner first, second sinned against." How does this change your approach to your relationships?

 If you missed this session, you can download the video teaching from *www.lifeway.com/Jonah*

Group Discussion

HEBREWS 3:12-14

Jonah, representing Israel, had forgotten the true grace of the God he served. The result was a hardening of his heart toward God and His purposes. The same predicament awaits anyone who allows the sins of pride, idolatry, and the like to reign in their heart and mind. In Hebrews 3:12-14, the author is writing to the Hebrew community urging them to not "fall away" (ESV) from God. The author is remembering the hard-heartedness of Israel when they refused to believe in God's love and trust in His power when they were called by God to take Canaan in Numbers 14. Instead of taking the land, the very people God had led out of Egypt by way of some amazing supernatural activity did not believe God would give them victory.

For Jonah, his ignorance of God's grace in his own life resulted in anger toward God and His purposes. For Israel at the border of Canaan, their ignorance of God's grace resulted in flat-out disobedience to His command. For both Israel and Jonah, the previous experience of God's grace in their own lives was not sustaining them in the present. As we study this brief passage in Hebrews, consider how we can keep from walking the same path Jonah, Israel, and so many others have walked in the past.

Read Hebrews 3:12-14.

> [12] Watch out, brothers, so that there won't be in any of you an evil, unbelieving heart that departs from the living God.
> [13] But encourage each other daily, while it is still called today, so that none of you is hardened by sin's deception.
> [14] For we have become companions of the Messiah if we hold firmly until the end the reality that we had at the start.

1. Verse 12 warns against departing from the living God. How does one "fall away" (ESV) from God?

2. Verse 13 says to exhort one another daily. What are we exhorting one another with?

3. Why might we need exhortation daily?
How does Jonah validate this?

4. How does a community of people help us deal with
our propensity toward ignorance of God's grace?

5. What could this look like in your small group?

6. What role does confession of sin play in
the church? What about in your life?

7. For Jonah, his anger toward God by the end of
Jonah 4 revealed what he really cared about. What are the
weighty rocks you care about right now in your life?

Wrap-Up

REVIEW

1. An idol is the one thing that has to be part of your future in order for life to be worth living.

2. When you see yourself as a recipient of great grace, then God's compassion becomes His most precious attribute to you, and you want to be like Him.

3. A person who understands God's grace toward them is continually amazed by how much of it they have in their life.

4. You are first a sinner to God and only second someone who is sinned against.

CHALLENGE

In the box below, write out one achievable action step you can take this week in response to what you've discussed in this group.

PRAY TOGETHER

Notes

PERSONAL STUDY

The personal study portion of the weekly guide is designed to take you on a slow walk through the Book of Jonah. The hope in doing this is you take time to consider what God is saying in these verses and what the implications are for your life. This week you will cover Jonah 4. As you walk through Jonah's dispute with God, take time to write some notes down and meditate on what God is saying to you.

1. The second prayer of Jonah. Jonah 4:1-3

In the wake of a remarkable act of God's mercy, the reader is led into an unexpected conversation between Jonah and God. Everything we know about narrative should make chapter 4 a resolution chapter. The drama should be over. Yet the chapter opens with Jonah displeased and "furious." Salvation comes to an entire nation, and a prophet of God is angry about it? Jonah's heart is revealed in his second prayer. In this prayer we find the heart behind his flight that began in Jonah 1. Jonah knew the character of God, and knew if God got involved with the evil nation of Nineveh, He might spare them. Jonah found Nineveh undeserving of God's grace and so he fled from God in hopes Nineveh would not be saved.

Though spoken in frustration, Jonah's recitation of the attributes of God creates a powerful picture of God for the reader, one any of us would do well to commit to memory. We must not be quick to overlook the God Jonah knows. What Jonah knew of God he saw on display in his own journey. The mercy and compassion of God brought Israel out of slavery. It is the God of Deuteronomy 4:31 of whom Moses says "He will not leave you, destroy you, or forget the covenant … because the LORD your God is a compassionate God." He is slow to become angry with the rebellious people He created to worship Him. He isn't just loving, He is rich in faithful love. And implied in His wealth of love is a generosity in giving that love to the human race. And last, He is not One who destroys, but One who relents from sending the disaster owed by sin. This is the

God of the Bible. And though Jonah is angry enough to ask for death, we will see that God extends His patience and love to Jonah.

Read back through the character of God Jonah describes. Spend time considering and perhaps writing down how knowing these attributes changes your approach to your personal situations.

Make it personal. Specifically looking at God's character as a model for our own, how does this passage call you to change the way you are currently interacting with your spouse, children, friends, etc.?

Go to *www.lifeway.com/Jonah* for a video devotion with Spence Shelton.

2. The angry prophet and the plant. Jonah 4:4-7

"Is it right for you to be angry?"

The question God asks Jonah penetrates Jonah's heart like a surgeon's scalpel. Is Jonah validated in his anger? What does his anger say about the condition of his heart? When one gets to a place where the mercy of God incites anger, have they replaced God as the arbiter of justice with themselves? God doesn't rebuke anger, for even He is angry at times. But God does call to question the motive of Jonah's anger and will teach Jonah more about mercy over the course of the next day.

The setting of the last scene in Jonah seems to be a somewhat desolate patch of land east of Nineveh. The reader gets the image of Jonah, stomping like a five-year-old who was denied a cookie by his parents, slamming materials around as he crafts what had to be a rather abysmal shelter to take shade in. While the king sits in ashes inside the city walls hoping to be spared, Jonah the man-child sits under his pile of sticks and waits futilely for the destruction of Nineveh that he knows God is not going to bring.

Just as God appointed a fish to deliver Jonah, now He appoints a plant to ease Jonah's suffering. And this is the only time we see Jonah smile in his entire journey. God saves Nineveh and Jonah pouts. God gives Jonah shade, and he rejoices. Notice the author is pointing to God's control over creation as he "appoints" the plant and then "appoints" the worm that attacks it. Our author never hesitates to remind us God has creation at the beckoning of His voice. As He appointed the plant, so also He appointed a worm to destroy the plant. On a patch of dirt within eyesight of His last act of mercy, God was dealing mercifully but intentionally with His prophet Jonah.

Is there anything you've ever been angry or
disappointed with God about? How is God's interaction
with Jonah relevant to your disappointment?

What might God be using in your life to remind
you of who He is and how He cares for you and
others? Pray and ask God for conviction on how
He may be calling you to respond to Him.

3. Jonah's lesson. Jonah 4:8-11

The final verses of the Book of Jonah put our main character in a heart corrective training session with his God. The quick withering of the shade-giving plant in 4:7 should elicit a response from Jonah similar to Job 1:21 where Job said after losing his entire family: "The LORD gives, and the LORD takes away. Praise the name of Yahweh." But after the sun beat down on Jonah's head to the point where he was fading from consciousness, Jonah retained his defiance toward God. He wanted to die. And this time, when God questioned whether Jonah was justified in his anger, Jonah finally let it out with a simple, sarcastic "Yes. It is right. I'm angry enough to die." Jonah was frustrated now both by the grace shown to Nineveh, and the removal of the grace God had shown to him in the plant. We find some sense of sympathy toward Jonah for a brief moment, for it does seem difficult at this point to understand how one could worship a God who saves his enemies but makes life miserable for his own prophet. That is, until we read God's reply in verses 10-11.

God contrasts Jonah's care for the plant with His own care for Nineveh. Jonah cared about that for which he did not labor. God is reminding Jonah very intentionally that he didn't deserve the grace given to him in the plant in the first place. God's description of the powerful, populous city of Nineveh as ignorant reinforces the spiritual eyes He is trying to get Jonah to see with. Yes, Nineveh was a powerful city in the Mediterranean world, but it was ignorant to what really mattered. Namely, they did not know and worship the one true God. If Jonah thought a plant was valuable, how much more valuable were 120,000 people created in the image of God! Jonah's lesson in the grace of God comes to an abrupt end here. God cares for the nations, including those who do not know Him, and will use even a frustrated, selfish, whining prophet to bring salvation to them.

Take a second and consider your time walking through Jonah. Having come to the end, what themes have stood out to you most?

How do you plan on applying those themes to your personal life going forward from here?

Week 6

A WHOLE NEW KIND
OF OBEDIENCE

INTRODUCTION

My (Spence) grandfather is known in my family for his one-liners. Pop has a knack, even in his upper 80s, for delivering a line. More times than not they come in the form of punch lines to some pretty entertaining jokes. For example, when we are playing golf together (yes he still gets out there regularly) he will watch me embarrass myself on a bad swing and quietly say, "Well, you hit the big ball (earth) before the little ball."

But Pop's most memorable lines are the ones that condense incredibly insightful advice into a powerful adage. Leading up to my wedding Pop was full of these for me. One that sticks with me still is when he said, "Spencer, the key to a long, strong marriage is to keep first things first and second things second." I've been married eight years as of the writing of this and I find that more true every day. It has become a consistent "aha" moment for me. Pop gets it when it comes to marriage, and he is passing his wisdom on to me. Instead of pouting over small things, I should make sure I'm spending my emotional and relational capital on the big things.

This is the advice Jonah needed to hear and to heed. As we come to the last part of Jonah's story, we see that his self-focus caused him to miss the big picture of what God was doing right in front of him. We hear a warning to fix our eyes on the big picture of God's mission lest we miss the great acts of grace happening before us.

GROUP STUDY

Warm-Up

**1. Can you think of a time where keeping the
big picture in mind was important?**

**2. This is our last session in this study. What idea,
realization, or anecdote is sticking with you to give you
a new understanding of the gospel according to Jonah?**

Video Setup

In this session J.D. will guide us through Jonah 4:5-11, the end of Jonah's
story. Notice Jonah's reaction to God's work in Nineveh and consider
what it reveals about him … and about you.

Play Video 6: "Obedience."

Video Guide

The Book of Jonah leaves us with a question: What do we _____

_____ _____?

Why do we have so much passion for things that really _____
_____ and so little passion for the things that _____ _____?

The repetition of _____ is there to underscore the greatness of
God's mission to save humanity.

Have you received this grace for yourself _____?

Has that experience of grace so transformed your heart that you have
become a person of _____ and _____?

Have you _____ your life priorities in light of the urgency
of that great mission?

You can either be part of the radical, self-sacrificial mission of Jesus, or
you can walk in _____ like Jonah.

Video Feedback

What out of this session, or this whole study, has stuck with you most?
What did you find most transformational?

What do you sense God calling you to in light of hearing and studying
the gospel message through the Book of Jonah?

 If you missed this session, you can download the
video teaching from *www.lifeway.com/Jonah*

Group Discussion

ROMANS 9:1-5

The apostle Paul was no slouch theologian. Inspired by the Holy Spirit, he penned some of the richest, most theologically deep thoughts ever recorded. In this passage we get a clear reminder that the things of God were not just mentally stimulating for Paul; he carried the gospel as his most important possession. He didn't just write about God, he treasured God. His words in Romans give stark contrast to the final words of Jonah in Jonah 4. Jonah lost sight of the grace shown to him. This brought about bitterness and selfishness instead of loving selflessness in his reactions to what God was doing.

Much like we have done in earlier sessions in this study, setting Jonah up against another key biblical figure (in this case Paul) provides a way to examine Jonah's heart and our own. One question to bear in mind during this session is, What should my life look like if it were marked by the same conviction in the gospel and compassion for my neighbors as Paul had?

Read Romans 9:1-5

¹ I speak the truth in Christ—I am not lying; my conscience is testifying to me with the Holy Spirit—² that I have intense sorrow and continual anguish in my heart. ³ For I could almost wish to be cursed and cut off from the Messiah for the benefit of my brothers, my own flesh and blood. ⁴ They are Israelites, and to them belong the adoption, the glory, the covenants, the giving of the law, the temple service, and the promises.
⁵ The ancestors are theirs, and from them, by physical descent, came the Messiah, who is God over all, praised forever. Amen.

1. Paul begins this section by saying "I am not lying" which he only does two other times in the New Testament. What does this tell us about what he is about to say?

2. Read verses 2-5 (see also 10:1). To dig into this we need to clear some things up. What do we know about Paul's "brothers" from his words here?

3. Contrast Paul and Jonah. What were their reactions to the state of those around them, and how were those reactions influenced by their knowledge of God?

4. Jonah wanted Nineveh to suffer while Paul wanted Israel to be redeemed. Why is Paul in such anguish? To put it another way, what does Paul get that Jonah is missing?

5. Why do you think we so often find ourselves reacting to God like Jonah in Jonah 4 instead of Paul in Romans 9 when it comes to the gospel? How do we grow beyond this?

6. How should the story of Jonah, and the fact that Paul is talking about Israelites, serve as a warning to those in the church today?

7. Reflect: What in your life do you care most about? What do you shed tears about?

8. How is Christ's great love for us, as seen in studying Jonah and these other places of Scripture, changing your response to Him?

Wrap-Up

REVIEW

1. The Book of Jonah leaves us with a question: What do we care most about?

2. We should have much passion for the things in life that really matter.

3. God's grace will transform your heart so that you become a person of compassion and generosity.

4. You should rearrange your life priorities in light of the urgency of God's great mission.

CHALLENGE

In the box below, write out one achievable action step you can take this week in response to what you've discussed in this group.

PRAY TOGETHER

Notes

PERSONAL STUDY

The personal study portion of the weekly guide is designed to take you on a slow walk through Scripture. The hope in doing this is you take time to consider what God is saying in these verses and what the implications are for your life. In this final week you will be studying Hebrews 9:11-28. As we heard earlier in the study, Jonah was a sign pointing to Jesus. Jesus is the new and better Jonah. The New Testament interprets the Old Testament through the events of Jesus' life, namely His death and resurrection. This week you will look at Hebrews 9 to see how Christ is the new and better sacrifice. You should leave this week with a little practice in seeing Christ in all of Scripture.

1. Once and for all. Hebrews 9:11-14

The Old Testament sacrificial system was designed to provide a way for the people of God to find forgiveness for their sins. The consequence of sin since it entered the garden of Eden is death. Sin is rebellion against God and so in cosmic justice the punishment of sin is death. In an act of mercy to spare people from death, God instituted the sacrificial system. An animal's death would stand in the place of the death of the one who sinned against God. Once a year the high priest of the Jewish people would go into the innermost room of the tabernacle, the dwelling place of God, and offer animal sacrifices on behalf of the entire nation. This would satisfy the judgment owed on an entire nation who needed rescue from the certain penalty they owed for their sin. Notice how one man would enter as a representative for all people. Romans 5:12 tells us sin entered the world through one man, Adam, and the penalty of death came with it. So we are not only personally guilty of sin, the human race is corporately guilty and in need of a Savior. So the priest entered the holy place as one man, a representative for all, to make payment for the sin of God's people.

This practice was foreshadowing, as Hebrews 9:14 alludes to, of what Christ's blood would do. Christ does not go back to the temple every year. He died once and His atonement covers all people for all times. The last words in verse 14 are that we are cleansed to "serve the living God." The response of one who has truly accepted grace is a life serving the God who gave it to him. This is not duty, but worship in response to the pardon he has received.

Hebrews 9 shows how this system was also a sign, pointing to a need for permanent salvation from sin for the people of God. The sign of Jonah is also the sign of the sacrificial system. In Christ the message of destruction for sin in Jonah is met with the hope of His death and resurrection. In Christ the message of death owed for sin in the sacrificial system is met in the once-and-for-all death of Christ and victory over it in His resurrection.

How does the author say the Messiah, Jesus, is different from the blood of animals? Why does this matter?

While we don't offer animal sacrifices, we do regularly try to justify ourselves before God through things other than Christ. How do you try to justify yourself before God?

How does the atonement of Christ personally set you free?

Go to *www.lifeway.com/Jonah* for a video devotion with Spence Shelton.

2. Christ's will. Hebrews 9:15-22

The New Testament writers regularly use legal language to help us understand our position before God. Concepts like penalties, justice, and in the case of this passage "will," help our finite minds begin to grasp the workings of an infinite God. Note this passage uses the word "will" in its less common biblical form referring to a legal document declaring certain people the inheritors of the property and rights owned by the individual. The word "will" does not refer directly to the sovereign purposes and autonomous activity of God Himself. (Indirectly this and everything else in the pages of the Bible are describing the will of God in this sense.)

This passage gives direct answer to a question I hear a lot: *Why did Jesus have to die?* Jesus' will created a new covenant for those who are "called." Now, instead of the death owed for their sin, they can have the promised eternal inheritance. This inheritance is life with God forever. It is a new heaven and a new earth where disease and violence are replaced by health and peace; where the world is ruled by a King who is just and good and who doesn't just allow us into the kingdom but adopts us as His sons and daughters. Why did Jesus have to die? Because until He died, as verse 17 says, His will was not in effect. So it's not that God wanted Jesus to die, it's that Jesus had to die for us to live.

Verse 22 highlights a central truth to understanding the gospel: We cannot work our way to salvation. We cannot do enough good works to earn the forgiveness of God for the sins we commit. Without the shedding of blood there is no forgiveness. And our predicament is that we as sinful people would be an unworthy sacrifice even if we sacrificed ourselves. Only the shedding of pure, innocent blood can bring about forgiveness. The author is showing us how it really is only Christ's blood that can forgive the debt owed by our sin.

Who is, or would be, the inheritors in your will?
What about those people gets them on your list?

How does, or could, knowing you are so loved
by God as to be in His will impact the way you
approach your life and those around you today?

3. The real thing. Hebrews 9:23-28

In this last section of our passage for this week the author pulls back the curtain to show us the reality of the cosmic implications of Christ's work on the cross and in the resurrection. This is no longer metaphorical language, but descriptive language of what actually took place and will take place through Christ. Before looking at those implications take a brief moment to survey what is happening in the scene painted by the author. These verses depict the judgment scene between God and Jesus the Messiah. The "copies" of the heavenly things are the tabernacle and the things in the tabernacle. Remember, the tabernacle represents the dwelling place of God. The true dwelling place of God is heaven where no man can go on his own. Jesus however went into the presence of God for us to stand in judgment for all people one time. Jesus took our place at the judgment seat.

The author acknowledges that each of us is appointed to die at some point and when we do, we face judgment from God. The Messiah has stepped into the judgment seat we are supposed to sit in. He bears the penalty of our sin in that seat. In doing so He brings salvation instead of judgment to those who are "waiting for Him." This waiting is a reference to the anticipation of the saints of Christ's return. Those who wait are the believers in Christ. This means we live with certain hope in the future reign of Christ.

In his shortsightedness Jonah had bitterness rather than hope. When you, however, see the glory of Christ and experience the grace of His sacrifice for you, you live with hopeful joy as you eagerly await the return of your King.

Spend some time thanking Jesus for His sacrifice
so that you might obtain eternal life. How will you
demonstrate your gratitude for Him today?

As you look forward to the second coming of
Christ, imagine the joy of standing in His presence.
What expressions of gratitude will you make?
What do you expect to hear from Jesus?

APPENDIX

Gospel Presentation

Evangelism is the process of engaging in a relationship with someone in a way that begins to expose them to the gospel and the Christian worldview. This process varies in each relationship. Sometimes the process is quick: God has already prepared their hearts and they are open to talking about their need for Christ. Other times, it takes years to help move unbelievers through their barriers to the gospel.

Evangelism is more than just the conversation in which a Christian shares the gospel with a non-Christian, but it is never less than clearly communicating how man's sin has devastated the world and separated him from God, and how the life, death, and resurrection of Jesus in our place is the only way to restore that broken relationship with God. Communicating the gospel clearly can feel like an overwhelming task. Below is a four-part framework designed to help make communicating the gospel a little less intimidating.

Creation → Fall → Redemption → Restoration

The whole Bible is a story about God's pursuit and rescue of mankind through Jesus. To share the gospel is simply to show someone how his or her story fits into God's story.

Below is a short synopsis of the story, and an example (in italics) of how you might explain each part of the story. Try doing the following to help learn this story enough so that you can retell it with ease:

1. *Memorize* the titles of the four parts to the story and the one-sentence summary thought attached to each title.
2. *Memorize* the Key Scriptures that accompany each one.
3. *Practice* re-drawing the illustrations provided with each step. We are a visual culture. Visualizing the story will be good for you as practice, and for those you share with to help capture the story. Whether or not you actually draw these illustrations will depend on the circumstances, but it's good to know in case you need it.

1. *Creation* – In the beginning, God created the world perfectly and man was in perfect relationship with Him.

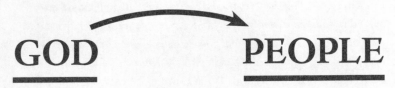

Genesis 1:27 says, "God created man in His own image; He created him in the image of God; He created them male and female."

Genesis 1:31 says, "God saw all that He had made, and it was very good."

Explanation: *God created everything, and it was "good." God, the Ruler and Creator of the universe, created people to know Him and have a relationship with Him. Everyone was in perfect relationship with each other and with God. The world was perfect; there was no sin, death, pain, stress, or disease. We [man] had a perfect sense of worth, purpose, security, and fulfillment in our relationship with God. This was the world as it should be.*

2. *Fall* – Man chose to sin, and our fellowship with God was broken. Man was separated from God.

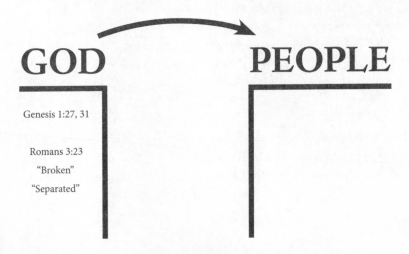

Romans 3:23: "For all have sinned and fall short of the glory of God."

Explanation: *Though created to follow and obey God like a son, Adam chose to rebel against God. That means that Adam chose his ways over God's ways. The Bible calls that rebellion sin. In that moment, sin broke everything and all of creation fell from a right relationship with God and each other (hence the term, "fall"). As a result of Adam and Eve's rebellion, there was an absence of peace, purpose, security, fulfillment, and joy. Adam and Eve became separated from God and were no longer in right relationship with Him.*

More Explanation: *In Genesis 3 (specifically 3:1-19), we see how Adam and Eve chose to rebel against God's authority and to try to find life, purpose, and fulfillment in themselves instead of in Him. Adam and Eve became separated from God and were no longer in right relationship with Him. Given that Adam and Eve were man's representatives, every human who would descend from Adam and Eve would bear the weight of the same curse as our predecessors. Romans 3:23 says, "For all have sinned and fall short of the glory of God." None of us is without sin. So today, we see a very different, broken world than the one that God originally created. Our relationships, sense of worth, sense of approval, security, purpose, and joy have all been ravaged by the devastating effects of sin. We now experience disease, pain, stress, natural disasters, and atrocities from man against man. In Romans 6:23, we see that "the wages of sin is death." The "death" referred to here is separation from God for all eternity in hell. Though we might try to do good things in an attempt to restore our relationship with God and earn our way to heaven, the Bible says in Isaiah 64:6 that "All of us have become like something unclean, and all our righteous acts are like a polluted garment." There is nothing that sinful man can do on his own to restore his broken relationship with God who is holy.*

3. **Redemption** – God knew that we could not save ourselves, so He sent His son Jesus Christ to live the perfect life that we should have lived, and then die the death that we deserved, to pay the penalty for our sin. Jesus is God's only provision for our sin.

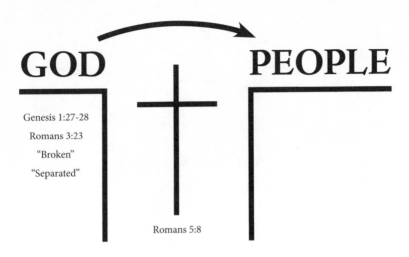

GOD   PEOPLE

Genesis 1:27-28
Romans 3:23
"Broken"
"Separated"

Romans 5:8

Romans 5:8: "God proves His own love for us in that while we were still sinners, Christ died for us!"

Explanation: *The good news of the gospel is that because God loves His people, He created a bridge to reconcile people to Himself. In John 14:6 Jesus says, "I am the way, the truth, and the life. No one comes to the Father except through Me." Romans 10:9 goes on to explain how we "come to God." It says that, "If you confess with your mouth, 'Jesus is Lord,' and believe in your heart that God raised Him from the dead, you will be saved."*

More Explanation: *God knew that we couldn't rescue ourselves from our sin and brokenness, and so He began unfolding His pursuit of mankind by bringing a Redeemer to rescue us! This culminated in the Person and work of Jesus Christ, God's only Son. Let's go back to Romans 6:23. This really helps to explain our brokenness and Christ's pursuit of us. The first half of the verse says, "the wages of sin is death." Man has earned death and separation from the only source of life found in Jesus Christ. The great news here is the second part of the verse: "but the gift of God is eternal life in Christ Jesus our Lord." Though we are separated from God, Jesus has made a way for us to be reconciled with God. Romans 5:8 says that "God proves His own love for us in that while we were still sinners, Christ died for us!" This means that Jesus took our place and was punished for our sin. He came and lived the perfect life we couldn't live, took the wrath of God for our sin in our place on the cross when He was killed, and then defeated sin and death in our place when He rose from the grave three days later. Now, Romans 10:9-10 shows us that all man has to do is to make the decision to confess and believe. The surrender of the control of our lives to Jesus leads to salvation, eternal life, and the joy of relationship with Christ (moving us from one side of the bridge to the other). Repenting means making the decision to relinquish the control of our own life, turn from finding life, purpose, security, and fulfillment in places other than Christ, and to submit to Jesus as the Lord of our life. "Confess" means to realize that there is nothing we can do to save ourselves, but that Jesus has done it all in our place. All we have to do to have our sin paid and atoned for is to confess who He is and believe what He did in His life, death, and resurrection. Those who make the decision to confess and believe receive the righteousness of Christ as their own and freedom from death (Romans 8:1-2).*

4. Restoration – It is not enough to simply understand these truths. Surrender to Christ is a personal decision. What God began in Jesus, he is completing in us. Jesus promises to give us a new life both now and forever. The story ends with God bringing people back to Himself.

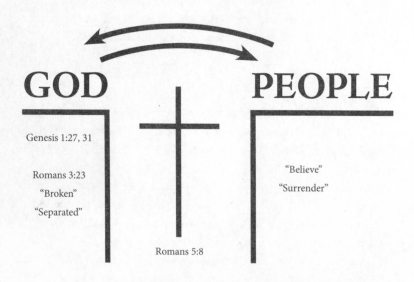

Explanation: *Now that God has made a way for man to be right with Him and redeemed through Christ, He is in the process of restoring all things. In Revelation 21:3-5 God shows us how one day He will take everything that is broken and restore it. Then we will be in heaven with God for eternity.*

**It is important to call the hearer to a decision. This means helping them see that the gospel isn't simply something that you believe for yourself, but rather a universal truth that applies to their life. Give them a chance to respond to the gospel with questions like, "Where on the bridge do you see yourself: on the side separated from God or on the side with God?" and "Which side of the bridge would you like to be on?" or "Would you like to make this decision to repent and trust Christ today?" Even if they respond that they are not ready to surrender the control of their life to Jesus, you have helped them to understand that the gospel is personal and that in order to be in right relationship with God, every man and woman must decide for themselves whether they will receive or reject God's authority and Christ's salvation. This line of questioning often reveals a person's personal barriers to the gospel, which then allows you to answer questions or enter into a process of helping them work through these barriers.

If you would like to surrender the control of your life to Christ, God is more concerned with the attitude of your heart than the words that you say. The following is a suggested prayer:

> God, I need You. I've been living for myself, and I want to surrender the control of my life to You and follow You for the rest of my life. Thank You for sending Jesus to take the penalty for my sin and restore my relationship with You! Take control of my life, and make me like You. I repent of my sins and place my trust in You.

LEADER GUIDE

Be sure to get *The Gospel According to Jonah* member books to your group members prior to the first session so that they can be prepared for your time together. Another option would be to have a preliminary meeting where books are passed out and the basic overview and flow of the study are given. You could view the Promo video together to boost enthusiasm for the study. This could be combined with another church event or informal get-together. Seek to establish a sense of belonging and accountability from the start!

Session 1 • I Am Jonah

In this session, J.D. teaches about Jonah's rebellion against God's command in chapter one of the Book of Jonah. We will hear how this depicts our own relationship with God, and how Christ meets us in our rebellion. Remember that there are leader training tips from Spence on the DVD.

Warm-Up: (10-15 min.) A few questions are provided to help members get comfortable talking within the group. Feel free to allow members to share their expectations and goals for this study if you sense God's leadership to modify the group time. Be sure to remind the group of the importance of their Personal Study time.

Watch Video Session 1: "Rebellion" (15:00).

Jonah had <u>personal</u> <u>bitterness</u> against Nineveh.

Rebellion is simply saying <u>"no"</u> to God.

If you want to <u>disobey</u>, there will always be a ship prepared to take you to Tarshish.

The downward progression of sin starts with <u>small</u> <u>disobedience</u> and ends in total spiritual disaster.

Our <u>disobedience</u> always affects others.

God sends storms into the lives of His people to wake them up from the <u>slumber</u> of sin.

That storm in your life is not there to <u>pay</u> you back for your sin, but to <u>bring</u> you back from your sin.

That storm is not designed for <u>retribution</u>; it's designed for <u>restoration</u>.

Video Feedback (15 min.) Review your notes from the video teaching and have group members share using the questions provided. It is important for them to be able to unpack what they have heard from J.D. and apply the truths to their lives.

Group Discussion (30 min.) These questions will facilitate discussion and help group members further apply principles from God's Word to their lives. Encourage members to share their stories as a source of encouragement to others.

Wrap-Up (5 min.) Restate the main purpose of this session. Encourage group members to complete their Personal Study and Challenge before the next meeting. Remember that there are video devotions from Spence at LifeWay.com/Jonah. Close in prayer.

Session 2 • The Futility of Life Without God

In this session, J.D. is going to look into the first half of Jonah's prayer in chapter two of the Book of Jonah. We are going to see what it took for Jonah to come to a place where he could finally obey God. Remember that there are leader training tips from Spence on the DVD.

Warm-Up: (10-15 min.) A few questions are provided to help members share from their Personal Study. Feel free to review other questions instead or allow members to share testimonies from the previous week if you sense God's leadership to modify the group time. Be sure to remind the group of the importance of their Personal Study time.

Watch Video Session 2: "Futility" (16:00).

The first major concept in Jonah's prayer of repentance is the futility of life without God.

Repentance always begins in a note of despair.

Better to be united with God even in the belly of a fish than on dry land without Him! The real pit is separation from God, not a particular circumstance.

The second major realization in Jonah's prayer is the emptiness of idols.

When you turn to an idol, you forfeit the grace that could be yours.

The third major realization in Jonah's prayer is salvation belongs to the Lord.

Seeing that Jesus was cast into the sea of God's wrath for us gives us the motivation for the new kind of obedience.

Video Feedback (15 min.) Review your notes from the video teaching and have group members share using the questions provided. It is important for them to be able to unpack what they have heard from J.D. and apply the truths to their lives.

Group Discussion (30 min.) These questions will facilitate discussion and help group members further apply principles from God's Word to their lives. Encourage members to share their stories as a source of encouragement to others.

Wrap-Up (5 min.) Restate the main purpose of this session. Encourage group members to complete their Personal Study and Challenge before the next meeting. Remember that there are video devotions from Spence at LifeWay.com/Jonah. Close in prayer.

Session 3 • Salvation Belongs to the Lord

In this session, J.D. guides the group to look into the end of Jonah's prayer, his message of salvation, and its implications for us. Remember that there are leader training tips from Spence on the DVD.

Warm-Up: (10-15 min.) A few questions are provided to help members share from their Personal Study. Feel free to review other questions instead or allow members to share testimonies from the previous week if you sense God's leadership to modify the group time. Be sure to remind the group of the importance of their Personal Study time.

Watch Video Session 3: "Salvation" (12:00).

Identify and describe the two ways J.D. says you have to read the Book of Jonah:

• <u>Existential</u>

• <u>Messianic</u>

All that the <u>prophet</u> Jonah did wrong, Jesus the <u>Messiah</u> did right.

Knowing that you might get swallowed by a fish if you disobey might change your <u>behavior</u>, but knowing Jesus was swallowed by death in your place will change your <u>heart</u>.

God isn't just after obedience; He's after a <u>whole</u> <u>new</u> <u>kind</u> of obedience, an obedience that grows from <u>desire</u>, an obedience fueled by <u>love</u>.

Being put in the belly of a whale can <u>coerce</u> your obedience; seeing Jesus went into the real belly of the whale is what creates <u>desire</u> in your heart.

Video Feedback (15 min.) Review your notes from the video teaching and have group members share using the questions provided. It is important for them to be able to unpack what they have heard from J.D. and apply the truths to their lives.

Group Discussion (30 min.) These questions will facilitate discussion and help group members further apply principles from God's Word to their lives. Encourage members to share their stories as a source of encouragement to others.

Wrap-Up (5 min.) Restate the main purpose of this session. Encourage group members to complete their Personal Study and Challenge before the next meeting. Remember that there are video devotions from Spence at LifeWay.com/Jonah. Close in prayer.

Session 4 • *The Making of a Witness*

In this session, J.D. will look at Jonah's journey to Nineveh where he preached God's Word and Nineveh responded. In Jonah we will see what is, and what is not, the responsibility of a witness. Remember that there are leader training tips from Spence on the DVD.

Warm-Up: (10-15 min.) A few questions are provided to help members share from their Personal Study. Feel free to review other questions instead or allow members to share testimonies from the previous week if you sense God's leadership to modify the group time. Be sure to remind the group of the importance of their Personal Study time.

Watch Video Session 4: "Witness" (17:00).

God blesses us to be a <u>blessing</u> to others.

Becoming an effective witness requires that you know two things:

1. <u>Salvation</u> belongs to the Lord (Jonah 2:9).

We're not dealing with skeptics who need to be <u>persuaded</u>; we are dealing with <u>dead</u> people who need to be <u>raised</u> to life.

2. <u>Faith</u> comes only by hearing (Romans 10:17).

The Word cannot do its work where people haven't <u>heard</u> it.

Knowing this should lead us to two things:

1. Get people in the presence of the <u>Word</u> <u>of</u> <u>God</u>.

2. <u>Pray</u> like crazy.

Video Feedback (15 min.) Review your notes from the video teaching and have group members share using the questions provided. It is important for them to be able to unpack what they have heard from J.D. and apply the truths to their lives.

Group Discussion (30 min.) These questions will facilitate discussion and help group members further apply principles from God's Word to their lives. Encourage members to share their stories as a source of encouragement to others.

Wrap-Up (5 min.) Restate the main purpose of this session. Encourage group members to complete their Personal Study and Challenge before the next meeting. Remember that there are video devotions from Spence at LifeWay.com/Jonah. Close in prayer.

Session 5 • The Problem with Religion

In this session, J.D. will look at the first half of the fourth and final chapter in the Book of Jonah. Here we will see how Jonah's idolatry and his ignorance created enmity between him and God. Again we will see God's patience and grace at work. Remember that there are leader training tips from Spence on the DVD.

Warm-Up: (10-15 min.) A few questions are provided to help members share from their Personal Study. Feel free to review other questions instead or allow members to share testimonies from the previous week if you sense God's leadership to modify the group time. Be sure to remind the group of the importance of their Personal Study time.

Watch Video Session 5: "Religion" (15:00).

An idol is the one thing that has to be part of your <u>future</u> in order for life to be worth living.

Jonah's two-fold disease:

1. Jonah is an <u>idolater</u>.

2. Jonah is <u>ignorant</u>.

When you see yourself as a recipient of great grace, then God's <u>compassion</u> becomes His most precious attribute to you, and you want to be like Him.

A person who understands <u>God's grace</u> in their life is continually amazed by how much of it they have in their life.

You are <u>first</u> a sinner to God and only <u>second</u> someone who is sinned against.

A spirit of <u>unforgiveness</u> and a lack of <u>generosity</u> is the indication you are out of touch with the grace of God in your own life.

Video Feedback (15 min.) Review your notes from the video teaching and have group members share using the questions provided. It is important for them to be able to unpack what they have heard from J.D. and apply the truths to their lives.

Group Discussion (30 min.) These questions will facilitate discussion and help group members further apply principles from God's Word to their lives. Encourage members to share their stories as a source of encouragement to others.

Wrap-Up (5 min.) Restate the main purpose of this session. Encourage group members to complete their Personal Study and Challenge before the next meeting. Remember that there are video devotions from Spence at LifeWay.com/Jonah. Close in prayer.

Session 6 • *A Whole New Kind of Obedience*

In this session, J.D. teaches through Jonah 4:5-11, the end of Jonah's story. Notice Jonah's reaction to God's work in Nineveh and what it reveals about him ... and about you. Remember that there are leader training tips from Spence on the DVD.

Warm-Up (10-15 min.) A few questions are provided to help members share from their Personal Study. Feel free to review other questions instead or allow members to share testimonies from the previous week if you sense God's leadership to modify the group time. Be sure to remind the group of the importance of their Personal Study time.

Watch Video Session 6: "Obedience" (17:00).

The Book of Jonah leaves us with a question: What do we <u>care</u> <u>most</u> <u>about</u>?

Why do we have so much passion for things that really <u>don't</u> <u>matter</u> and so little passion for the things that <u>actually</u> <u>do</u>?

The repetition of <u>"great"</u> is there to demonstrate the greatness of God's mission to save humanity.

Have you received this grace for yourself <u>personally</u>?

Has that experience of grace so transformed your heart that you have become a person of <u>compassion</u> and <u>generosity</u>?

Have you <u>rearranged</u> your life priorities in light of the urgency of that great mission?

You can either be part of the radical, self-sacrificial mission of Jesus, or you can walk in <u>disobedience</u> like Jonah.

Video Feedback (15 min.) Review your notes from the video teaching and have group members share using the questions provided. It is important for them to be able to unpack what they have heard from J.D. and apply the truths to their lives.

Group Discussion (30 min.) These questions will facilitate discussion and help group members further apply principles from God's Word to their lives. Encourage members to share their stories as a source of encouragement to others.

Wrap-Up (5 min.) Restate the main purpose of this session. Encourage group members to complete their Personal Study and Challenge even though this is the final group meeting. You might also discuss which Bible study you will want to study next if your group will be staying together. Remember that there are video devotions from Spence at LifeWay.com/Jonah. Close in prayer.

END NOTES

1. Jeffery M. Jones, "Barack Obama, Hillary Clinton Again Top Most Admired List," Gallup Politics [online], 27 Dec. 2011 [cited 7 Sept. 2012]. Available from the Internet: *www.gallup.com/poll/151790/barack-obama-hillary-clinton-again-top-admired-list.aspx.*

2. Howard Taylor, *Borden of Yale* (Philadelphia: China Inland Mission, 1926) 75.

3. Jon Wilke, "Churchgoers Believe in Sharing Faith, Most Never Do." LifeWay [online], 13 Aug. 2012, [cited 7 Sept. 2012]. Available from the Internet: *www.lifeway.com/Article/research-survey-sharing-christ-2012.*

4. Sinclair Ferguson, *Man Overboard* (Carlisle, PA Banner of Truth Publishing 1981) 51.

5. "Japanese diners hospitalized after eating bad fugu" *NY Daily News* [online], 27 Jan. 2009 [cited 19 Sept. 2012]. Available from the Internet: *http://articles.nydailynews.com/2009-01-27/news/17915241_1_blowfish-poisoning-fugu-hospitalized.*

WELCOME TO COMMUNITY!

Meeting together to study God's Word and experience life together is an exciting adventure. A small group is a group of people unwilling to settle for anything less than redemptive community.

Core Values

Community: God is relational, so He created us to live in relationship with Him and each other. Authentic community involves sharing life together and connecting on many levels with others in our group.

Group Process: Developing authentic community takes time. It's a journey of sharing our stories with each other and learning together. Every healthy group goes through stages over a period of months or years. We begin with the birth of a new group, then deepen our relationships in the growth and development stages.

Interactive Bible Study: God gave the Bible as our instruction manual for life. We need to deepen our understanding of God's Word. People learn and remember more as they wrestle with truth and learn from others. Bible discovery and group interaction enhance growth.

Experiential Growth: Beyond solely reading, studying, and dissecting the Bible, being a disciple of Christ involves reunifying knowledge with experience. We do this by taking questions to God, opening a dialogue with our hearts (instead of killing desire), and utilizing other ways to listen to God speak (other people, nature, art, movies, circumstances). Experiential growth is always grounded in the Bible as God's primary revelation and our ultimate truth-source.

Power of God: Processes and strategies will be ineffective unless we invite and embrace the presence and power of God. In order to experience community and growth, Jesus needs to be the centerpiece of our group experiences and the Holy Spirit must be at work.

Redemptive Community: Healing best occurs within the context of community and relationships. It's vital to see ourselves through the eyes of others, share our stories, and ultimately find freedom from the secrets and lies that enslave our souls.

Mission: God has invited us into a larger story with a great mission of setting captives free and healing the broken-hearted (Isaiah 61:1-2).

However, we can only join in this mission to the degree that we've let Jesus bind up our wounds and set us free. Others will be attracted to an authentic redemptive community.

Sharing Your Stories

The sessions of *The Gospel According to Jonah* are designed to help you share a bit of your personal life with the other men in your group as you experience life together. Through your time together, each member of the group is encouraged to move from low risk, less personal sharing to higher risk communication. Real community will not develop apart from increasing intimacy over time.

Sharing Your Lives

As you share your lives together during this time, it's important to recognize that it's God who brought each man to this group, gifting the individuals to play a vital role in the group (1 Corinthians 12:1). Each of you was uniquely designed to contribute in your own unique way to building into the lives of the other men in your group. As you get to know one another better, consider the following four areas that will be unique for each person. These areas will help you get a "grip" on how you can better support others and how they can support you.

G – Spiritual Gifts God has given you unique spiritual gifts
(1 Corinthians 12; Romans 12:3-8; Ephesians 4:1-16).
R – Resources You have resources that perhaps only you can share, including skill, abilities, possessions, money, and time (Acts 2:44-47; Ecclesiastes 4:9-12).
I – Individual Experiences You have past experiences, both good and bad, that God can use to strengthen and encourage others
(2 Corinthians 1:3-7; Romans 8:28).
P – Passions There are things that excite and motivate you. God has given you those desires and passions to use for His purposes (Psalm 37:4,23; Proverbs 3:5-6,13-18).
To better understand how a group should function and develop in these four areas, consider taking your group on a journey in community using the LifeWay Small Groups study entitled *Great Beginnings*.

LEADING A SMALL GROUP

You will find a great deal of helpful information in this section that will be crucial for success as you lead your group.

Reading through this section and utilizing the suggested principles and practices will greatly enhance the group experience. First is to accept the limitations of leadership. You cannot transform a life. You must lead your group to the Bible, the Holy Spirit, and the power of Christian community. By doing so your group will have all the tools necessary to draw closer to God and to each other, and to experience heart transformation.

Make the following things available at each session:

+ *The Gospel According to Jonah* member book for each attendee
+ Extra Bibles and pens or pencils for each attendee
+ Snacks and refreshments (encourage everyone to bring something)

The Setting and General Tips

1. Prepare for each meeting by reviewing the material, praying for each group member, asking the Holy Spirit to join you, and making Jesus the centerpiece of every experience.
2. Create the right environment by making sure chairs are arranged so each person can see every other attendee. Set the room temperature at 69 degrees. If meeting in a home, make sure pets are where they cannot interrupt the meeting. Request that cell phones be turned off. Have music playing softly as people arrive.
3. Try to have soft drinks and coffee available for early arrivals.
4. Have someone with the spiritual gift of hospitality ready to make any new attendees feel welcome.
5. Be sure there is adequate lighting so that everyone can read easily.
6. Think of ways to connect with group members away from group time. The amount of participation you have during your group meetings is directly related to the amount of time you connect with your group members away from the group meeting. Consider sending e-mails, texts, or social networking messages during the week encouraging

them to come next week and to expect God to do great things throughout the course of this study.

7. There are four types of questions used in each session: Observation (What is the passage telling us?), Interpretation (What does the passage mean?), Self-revelation (How am I doing in light of the truth unveiled?), and Application (Now that I know what I know, what will I do to integrate this truth into my life?). You may not be able to use all the questions in each study, but be sure to use some from each.

8. Don't lose patience about the depth of relationship group members are experiencing. Building authentic Christian community takes time.

9. Be sure pens or pencils are available for attendees at each meeting.

10. Never ask someone to pray aloud without asking them first.

Leading Meetings

1. Before the Review sections, do not say, "Now we're going to do a review." The entire session should feel like a conversation from beginning to end, not a classroom experience.

2. Be certain every member responds to the small-group questions. The goal is for every person to hear his or her own voice early in the meeting. People will then feel comfortable to converse later on. If members can't think of a response, let them know you'll come back to them after the others have spoken.

3. Remember, a great group leader talks less than 10 percent of the time. If you ask a question and no one answers, just wait. If you create an environment where you fill the gaps of silence, the group will quickly learn they don't need to join you in the conversation.

4. Don't be hesitant to call people by name as you ask them to respond to questions or to give their opinions. Be sensitive, but engage everyone in the conversation.

5. Don't ask people to read aloud unless you have gotten their permission prior to the meeting. Feel free to ask for volunteers to read.

6. Watch your time. If discussion extends past the time limits suggested, offer the option of pressing on into other discussions or continuing the current content into your next meeting.

REMEMBER: People and their needs are always more important than completing your agenda or finishing all the questions.

Lose your religion.

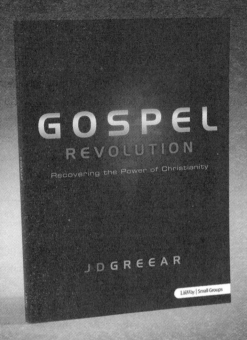

GOSPEL
REVOLUTION

Recovering the Power of Christianity

J D G R E E A R

LifeWay | Small Groups

This eight-session Bible study will lead you and your group to understand how to let the gospel work in your heart the way religion never has, or ever could. The good works we all try (and often fail) to do come naturally when we are simply captivated by the love of Christ. To learn more, go to lifeway.com/gospel or call 800.458.2772.

 Scan the QR code to watch an interview with J.D. about the Gospel Movement.

Biblical Solutions for Life

DO YOU GO WHEREVER HE LEADS YOU?

Author of the *New York Times* Best Seller **RADICAL**

FOLLOW ME

BIBLE STUDY

DAVID PLATT

DVD | LifeWay

Are you a follower of Christ? Are you sure? When Jesus says, "Come, follow Me," it is not an invitation to say a prayer. It is a summons to lose our lives. But have we? In this much-anticipated follow-up to *Radical*, David Platt continues to challenge cultural Christianity. And it just might challenge you and your entire church. So get with your group. Watch Platt on video. Take some time to retreat, reflect, and genuinely respond to Jesus' invitation, "Follow Me."

lifeway.com/followme | 800.458.2772 | LifeWay Christian Stores

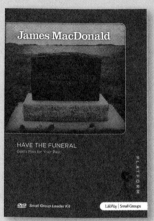
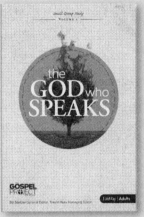
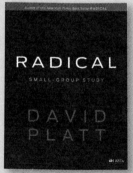
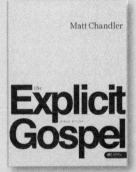

GROUP DIRECTORY

Write your name on this page. Pass your books around and ask your group members to fill in their names and contact information in each other's books.

Your Name: _____

Name: _____   Name: _____
Phone: _____   Phone: _____
E_Mail: _____   E_Mail: _____
Social Network(s): _____   Social Network(s): _____

Name: _____   Name: _____
Phone: _____   Phone: _____
E_Mail: _____   E_Mail: _____
Social Network(s): _____   Social Network(s): _____

Name: _____   Name: _____
Phone: _____   Phone: _____
E_Mail: _____   E_Mail: _____
Social Network(s): _____   Social Network(s): _____

Name: _____   Name: _____
Phone: _____   Phone: _____
E_Mail: _____   E_Mail: _____
Social Network(s): _____   Social Network(s): _____

Name: _____   Name: _____
Phone: _____   Phone: _____
E_Mail: _____   E_Mail: _____
Social Network(s): _____   Social Network(s): _____

Name: _____   Name: _____
Phone: _____   Phone: _____
E_Mail: _____   E_Mail: _____
Social Network(s): _____   Social Network(s): _____